# The Locket
# and
# A Five Taka Note

By

Catherine M. Byrne
with
Abdul Mkith

D1362877

Published by

Fireflash Publishing
Bagend, Roadend, Stanstill,
Watten, Wick. Caithness.
KW1 5UN

www.fireflashpublishing.co.uk


Cover by SelfPubBookCovers.com/Shardel

To Patsy and Freddy Anderson.
All I am today, I owe to you.

## Author's note

In October 2012, an English teacher contacted me. He told me he had been working with a boy who was keen to tell his tale to the world. I met with Abdul, then twenty-four, and was immediately drawn to this personable and attractive young man. Bit by bit he told me his story and supplied me with the notes that the authorities held on him.

Names of individuals have been changed, but otherwise *The Locket and A Five Taka Note* is his true story, as he told it to me.

Catherine M Byrne

# The Locket
# And
# A Five Taka Note

Foreword

My name is Abdul Mkith. I was born in Borlekha in
Syhlet, Bangladesh. My father owned a shop where he
sold a variety of things and he made furniture and bricks.
He was the richest man in the village, and the most
respected. My mother is my father's second wife.

I have three brothers and two sisters. At the time of my
story, apart from myself, one brother and one sister
remain at home. Our household consists of my parents,
our servant, Jasmine, our personal Imam, and us three
siblings.

# Prologue

## Scotland 2010

*I am startled into wakefulness by a pounding at the door. My first thought is that Hoss has returned. I leap out of bed and poise with the knife raised. A voice shouts, 'Police, open up.' I trust nothing and no one now. I do not know whether this is the British police or another of Hoss's stunts. I only hope the lock will hold.*

*Then comes the sound of breaking glass and two figures burst in through the window. When I see their white skin and uniforms, I realise this really is the British police; that one way or another I am going to escape Hoss's clutches. Lowering the knife I smile in relief. In my heart I am grateful for this intervention, no matter what it might lead to.*

*They back away. 'He's got a knife,' one says. I realise at that moment how I must look, standing there, covered in blood, clutching a knife and grinning like an idiot, the sheet trailing behind me, stuck to my body by dried blood. I fling the knife from me and hold up my hands the way I've seen it done in the movies. One of the policemen leaps forward, yanks my arms down, twists them behind my back and hurls me face down on the bed. I think my arms are going to be dragged from their sockets. Straddling me, he handcuffs me and tightens the cuffs until they stop my circulation. The pain is unbearable.*

*A pretty policewoman comes in. 'What are you doing?' she shouts. 'That's only a kid.'*

*The constable gives a snort. 'So what? He's one of them.'*

# Chapter One
# Scotland
# 2006

Today the sunshine is fragile and gives little heat. I sit on the cliff-top among pink thrift and straggly daisies in this damp green place that I have made my home, staring over the crinkled blue of the sea. To my left is the ocean, stretching as far as the eye can see. Away to the right is a ruined castle, remnant of a heritage that will never be mine.

Turning the collar of my jacket up against the bite of the wind, I watch vessels glide silently past or materialize from the blur where the sea and the sky become one. Gulls swoop and cry above my head and, as the water races over the shingle on the beach rattling the pebbles and throwing white spray up the cliff face, my mind carries me back to another place, another world. A world where the music is of hot breezes through flat, glossy palm leaves, the song of birds in the early morning and the call to prayer from the mosques. A world where the air is hot and dry and dusty. A place where even the flies are lazy.

It is September. Back home the people from my village will be flooding the fields before transplanting the dhan from where it grows lime-green and waist-high to a place where it will have room to spread and produce and deepen and eventually ripen into milk-white paddy, ready to be harvested. The farmers will have clubbed together to hire a pump to transport water from our rivers.

Had I been there now I would be calf-deep in water, pushing the plants into the silt, a short distance apart. At home Ammo will be cooking, the aromas filling the spaces of our house. Later the families will wash before prayer and, afterwards, gather together to eat and laugh and gossip.

How I wish I could be with them now.

Today I am eighteen. At least I have been told I am eighteen. When I was rescued I could not tell them when I had been born. In my culture people pay little attention to the exact year of their birth. We are more likely to remember the events of that time, like floods or earthquakes.

In the UK, eighteen is the date which marks a child's passage into adulthood. The date when he or she is free to choose his own path in life, when he is eligible to vote for who should govern the country, when he may walk into a public house and order a drink of alcohol, when he can smoke, gamble and open his own bank account or go to university and follow the career of his choosing; the date that I am free to return to the land of my birth if I so choose or the authorities decide to send me. Only, I have been told that my parents are dead and it is my fault. They have been murdered because I refused to return to my captors. I close my eyes against the pain and let my memory carry me back through the years.

# Chapter 2
# Bangladesh 1998

As usual I am the last to wake up. Morning light, milky through the mosquito net, fills the space around me. The voices of my family jabber over the early food and the aromas of fresh bread, garlic, ginger and coriander waft through the house.

'Abdul! Rise, rise, get up, lazy boy,' my mother, my ammo, shouts. Her voice is always louder than the rest. Her voice is the strongest thing about her. I pull the cover over my face, but she is here, screeching at me, pulling the net aside with her small hands, dragging at my arms. She is near enough for me to see the spidery lines around her eyes and furrows running down either side of her thin lips and to smell the spices she uses. 'Get up you lazy boy. You will make everyone late for prayer.'

'I'll get him up.' My brother, Bahir, eases her to one side. He is already taller than my father and his arms, after years of farm work, are thick and strong. He drags the covers away and slaps me. His hand is hot and dry and rough. Kicking and yelling, I try to fight him off. Sleep still claims me.

'Leave the boy alone. I will bring him,' my father, my abboo shouts from the room where we sit to eat on the carpeted floor.

'No, you will stay and have your food,' my mother orders.

My father owns a furniture shop in the village and will be leaving after prayers.

'I'll wake him up,' says a soft voice. My sister, lovely A'isha, comes in and shoos the others away. At thirteen

10

she is almost a woman, small and neat like Ammo with the same large, almond-shaped eyes. In her hand she carries a plate of food which she sets by the bed. One finger is smeared with tooth powder. 'Come,' she says, lifting my head and helping me to sit. 'Open your mouth.' She cleans my teeth with her finger. Then she feeds and dresses me. Since the day I was born, I have been her doll, her special little one. Although I am capable of doing these things myself, I am quite happy to let her pamper me.

'Come, child,' says my father, while my mother and brother grumble about how he spoils me. With little effort, he lifts me onto his shoulders and carries me to the first prayer of the day.

I am nine years old.

We have a private mosque a short way from the house. Abboo provides our Imam, our spiritual leader, with food and shelter in return for his services. After morning prayers, he teaches us about Islam; about our prophet and how to pray; how we must love one another, our parents and people of all nations. But I can never sit still. I cannot concentrate and all the time I fidget. The sun is climbing and dappling through the leaves of the palm trees and the birds are beginning to sing. A welcome breeze from the open window wafts across my skin and the outdoors call to me. I want to play cricket until the sun sinks and our shadows grow long and thin, I want to splash in the pond at the bottom of our garden where we wash, I want to run in the fields, drive the cattle round the yard so that they trample the paddy stalks to separate the rice, climb trees – even lie on my bedroll, anything except sit in a classroom. As my dreams carry me to distant planes, the voice of our teacher dulls to a drone of meaningless noise.

'You – Abdul,' shouts the Imam, grabbing a bamboo cane he keeps at his side. He comes towards me, his eyes dark pools of anger, shaggy brows meeting in the middle. His fingers tighten around the cane and it swishes up and back. The Imam has the right to beat me if he chooses and he has done so in the past. It makes no difference whether he does or not, sitting still is impossible for me. Raising my arms, I cower from the threat, but this time he lowers the cane and orders me to sit with my head between my knees as a punishment.

As soon as the lesson is over, I am the first person to run out of the door followed by warning shouts from the Imam. Outside is sunshine, soft breezes, freedom.

'Abdul,' my sister says as she catches up with me. 'I hate seeing you get into trouble. Why don't you pay attention?'

'I don't like lessons,' I tell her. I giggle and run from her. She chases me back to the house and together we crash through the door, laughing.

Jasmine, a poor girl my parents have taken from the streets and provided with a home in return for help in the house and fields, prepares our food while we go to the pond to wash. My mother is resting; her health is not good.

It is left to my sister to see that I go to school. We walk along the road, our bare feet sending puffs of dust from the beaten track. On either side, the farmers work in the paddy fields; it is December, the month of the harvest. 'Ah, Abdul, you go to school,' they shout to me. 'You will be a wise man one day.'

Hired carts wait at the edge of the fields to be filled with the dhan, the rice stalks, which then will be brought into the yard to be separated from the grains. Had I not gone to school, like some boys I know who are too poor for education, I would have helped to drive the sleek brown cattle across the stalks and helped to collect the rice for processing, I would have gathered up the straw to use

12

as animal feed in times of drought. I envy these boys their freedom, but Abboo wants his children to learn. He never tires of telling us how important knowledge is for the girls as well as the boys. He is not like many men of our culture who believe education is wasted on a girl since her role in life is to be married and produce children.

The path is lined with mango trees, their leaves offering a dappled shade. Away to the north, beyond the low-roofed buildings of the village, beyond the patchwork of chilli, mustard, and rice fields there are mountains, blued by distance.

The school is a long, squat building, at the edge of the village, surrounded by a fence. There are two doors, one for the older children and one for my age group. A'isha goes to big school, so she leaves me outside the gates. 'Make sure you go to class today or Bahir will find out and beat you,' she says. Her friends see her and wave and I am alone. I walk slowly towards the school door. A'isha glances over her shoulder and smiles. I return that smile. She is satisfied.

'Abdul, are you coming to class today?' shouts a boy as he joins the queue of kids with whom I play cricket. Each child has a hand on the shoulder of the one in front, waiting to snake into the building. I shake my head. He does not look surprised.

Once the big school has swallowed A'isha and she cannot see me, I turn and run down the dusty road before the teacher opens the door and maybe catches sight of me. I run all the way to the village and my father's shop. Inside smells of sawdust and resin. My father is turning a chair-leg on a lathe. Golden twists of shavings curl and fall, joining a heap on the ground. His assistant stands over another bench, sanding a length of wood held in a vice. He runs his hand over the smooth surface and blows the dust away. Flies buzz in the air.

'Abdul,' Abboo says. 'What are you doing here?'

'I need five taka,' I tell him.

'Why do you need five taka?'

'I have to get a new pencil case. My teacher told me.'

'But I gave you money for a new pencil case last week.' He goes to his cash register and it rings as he punches a button and the drawer slides open. He gives me five taka anyway. My father denies me nothing.

Twenty minutes' walk takes me to our nearest town, Bazar. As I weave between the rickshaws, the constant blare of car horns and shouting from the stalls fill my ears. I skirt around the goods for sale outside the shop fronts. No one takes notice of me in this busy town. There is a place I know, the picture-house where they show films, both Bollywood and American, once a day, illegally, on a television and VCR. It is a small room, hot and airless, with fourteen or fifteen people crowded together. I pay my five taka to the man at the door and find a seat just as the film is about to start. I dodge my head this way and that to see the screen around a tall man who sits in front of me. One day I'll become a star myself. The hero's face fills the screen and I imagine myself in that role, or maybe singing and dancing on the stage. This is what I want to do.

Once the film is over, I need to fill in time until the end of the school day. I walk around the bazaar where the merchants sit at their stalls. Everywhere there are wares set out for sale; fruit, vegetables, pans, clothes, fish, chickens, frogs struggling in buckets. And the smell of food, spices and flowers. When I grow bored, I go to the train station to watch men and women come and go. There are crowds everywhere. They walk across the lines until the train comes, its horn blowing a warning. So many carriages, all blue and cream, they seem to go on forever. Boys and men ride on the outside, clinging to whatever they can, or climbing onto the roof, anything to get to their destination.

Many times I have watched the carriages draw into the station, people getting on and getting off. I long to know where the train takes them, what it is like to travel on the great iron monster with its clacking wheels. Today, I creep on board and find myself in a long corridor with bodies filling the spaces, jolting me aside, crushing into seats, yacking at each other with loud voices. The guard blows his whistle. Suddenly I am afraid. I squeeze through the throng, desperate to get out before the train begins to move. Reaching the door, I dash through before it closes. The guard shouts and tries to slap my head, but I run and run. I am good at running.

Every day I meet A'isha after classes and she does not know I have missed school, but today, as I reach the school gate, I see my father striding towards me. 'Abdul,' he says. 'why are you out of class?' His voice is stern.

'We closed early today,' I say, my voice shivering with the lie.

'You are playing truant again. You had better not let your mother and brother find out.'

Abboo will not scold me. I am the youngest, the favoured child.

'May I come with you?' I ask.

'Ah, Abdul. What am I to do with you? You must stop this running out of school. You know education is important.' Abboo lifts me onto his broad shoulders. His arms are thick and I feel as light as air in his hands.

My father is well respected in the village – a man who built up his business from nothing. Once he walked from door to door and through the streets of Bazar selling his goods; now he owns a carpenter's shop, several acres of land, a dozen head of cattle and a long, five-roomed house built from the brick he also makes and sells. These bricks are made of clay and fired in a kiln.

15

We are the only family in the village to have electricity, and a television gifted by a customer who couldn't pay his bill. Every evening, Abboo sets the TV outside and all the villagers bring their chairs and sit to watch the programs. Ammo and Jasmine bring them food. I am so proud of my father.

Because he is known for his fairness, Abboo is called upon to settle disputes in the village. As we walk, he holds onto my feet, and my fingers entwine in his hair, still thick and black, although his face shows the years he has been on this earth. He tells me about this latest case.

'There are bad men,' he says, 'Mafia gangsters who try to make everyone afraid of them. They make money illegally and help support those in high places. Because of this they will never go to prison. Now one of them, his name is Kamal, has decided he wants a Hindu girl because of her beauty. The girl's family want him to leave her alone. They have come to me for help.'

'But what can you do?' I ask.

'I will do what I believe is right. The villagers respect me. They will uphold my decision.'

We come to the yard where both sides wait for my father to arrive. There are two rows of chairs facing each other with a chair at the end, facing down. This is where Abboo sits. He takes me on his knee. Both sides are shouting, voices so raised I cannot make out what they are saying. Abboo demands quiet. His voice is loud and strong and booms above the rest, forcing them to silence. He wants to listen to the story from both sides.

The girl's father, Mr Kumar, stands up. 'My daughter,' he says, 'she is promised to a boy of her own religion. They are to be married in two months. She does not want this man from the village. Yet he follows her, says rude things to her, touches her. She is afraid to go out alone. Then he stands outside my house and watches her.'

Kamal stands up. He shakes his fist at the Kumars. 'Why should I not have her? Why should she be forced to marry against her will?' Then his family rise from their seats and the shouting from both sides start again.

'It is her will and the will of the family that she marries a man of her own religion.' Her father's words, shaking like reeds in the wind, climb beyond the commotion.

Then all the voices rise together so it is impossible to make out individual words. Fists are shaken, fingers pointed.

Abboo calls for quiet and once the noise abates, he asks the girl, 'Is it true? Do you want this boy?'

She does not raise her eyes. Her hands twine together. A tear on her cheek catches the sun. She shakes her head.

'And is it true you are afraid of him?'

She glances at Kamal, presses her lips into a thin line and nods. 'Yes. I want him to stop,' she whispers in a voice so quiet I barely hear her.

'And do you want to marry the boy your parents have chosen for you?'

'Yes, sir, I do,' she says, still looking at her lap.

Everyone starts to shout again. The air is filled with voices.

Abboo claps his hands. 'Enough.' His eyes turn to Kamal. 'You will leave her alone and apologise to the family for the distress you have caused them.' His voice is solid and rises above the melee. The others fall silent. All eyes turn to Kamal.

Kamal's father nods. 'We accept your ruling,' he says.

'Well, I do not,' shouts Kamal. 'I will not apologise. You will not tell me what I will do, old man.' He turns on his father, shocking me with his lack of respect. 'Why should I apologise to her? She is a dirty Hindu – worth nothing.'

My father is angry. His body stiffens beneath me. 'It is written in the holy Qur'an, "You shall have your religion and I shall have my religion." What does it matter if she is a Hindu? She has the same rights as you.'

Kamal points his finger at Mr Kumar and his wife. 'You will be sorry,' he shouts, then turns to my father. 'You have chosen to support a Hindu against your Muslim brothers. I have many friends who will not tolerate this.' Then he looks at me and laughs – not a nice laugh, and says, 'Take care of your son.'

'The ruling remains.' Abboo stands up. 'Come on, Abdul, let us go home.'

I trot along beside him, Kamal's threats already forgotten.

# Chapter 3

A week later, I was pulled from sleep by shouting and the room was filled with a flickering light and the smell of burning. I jumped out of bed and fought off the mosquito net in my hurry. Leaning out of the window, I coughed as the smoke rolled towards me in a black wrathful cloud. Down the street I saw flames leaping up, filling the sky. Figures, black against angry red, running, screaming, shouting. It took a few minutes to realise it was the house of Mr and Mrs Kumar. I gripped the wood around the window until my fingers hurt. Chandraj Kumar was my friend; we played cricket together. His lovely sister, Asmita, and all the family – where they still inside? Fear for their safety held me in an iron grip. The smell of burnt wood thickened in my nostril. The panic and the fear remain in my mind till this day. Silhouetted figures came towards our house, the red glow all around them. Closer to, I recognised Abboo leading Mr Kumar and Chandraj. Mrs Kumar and Asmita came behind, coughing, blankets wrapped around their bodies and covering their faces. I thanked Allah they had escaped.

I ran to meet them.

'The whole family will be welcome to stay under our roof,' Abboo said. 'Chandraj will sleep with you on your bed-roll.' His voice was tight, angry, his eyes screwed down, the muscles of his neck rigid. Mr Kumar's face was still. He stared past me. His wife moved her head from side to side, wailing low in her throat. Asmita made no sound but clung to her mother.

As soon as she entered our house, Mrs Kumar burst into tears. 'We have nothing left,' she sobbed. 'Everything – all my mother's jewellery – they have taken my life.'

My ammo wrapped the hysterical woman in her arms. 'You must not worry. You will be safe here.'

Jasmine brought them a drink of water.

'We know who did this,' Abboo said, as the crack and roar of collapsing timbers filled the night and sparks lit up the sky.

'But what can we do? We are powerless against those people.' Mr Kumar stared at the wall, tears running freely down his face. 'I now am afraid for your family.'

'Do not worry about us,' said Abboo. 'I am well respected here. They won't dare harm us.'

Sobbing, Asmita bandaged Mr Kumar's hands which were red and black and blistered.

'It's too late.' His wife gave a low moan as she stared out of the window. 'The fire is too fierce. Everything has gone. All my things, my lovely things, things passed down to me by my mother and her mother before her.'

After the flames had quietened and the remains of their home crumbled and fell and settled and only ribboning smoke, errant flares and the stench of charred wood and dust remained, I climbed onto my bed-roll and lay on the edge so that there was room for Chandraj. He trembled beneath the cover and cried. His face was streaked and black. 'They tried to kill us,' he said over and over.

'Do not worry; Abboo has power. He will look after you,' I whispered.

I believed back then that my father had the power to do anything.

Next day, after morning prayer, instead of going to the fields, the men from the village, Muslim and Hindu and Christian arrived at our door. So many of them came that they walked like an army bearing hammers and tools of every kind.

'Why are they not in the fields?' I asked A'isha as she rubbed oil into my hair.

'They have come for leadership from Abboo. They want to build a new house for the Kumars,' she said.

In the yard Abboo was smiling. 'You see,' he patted Mr Kumar on the shoulder, 'you have many friends.'

Mr Kumar sniffed and wiped his red eyes on his bandaged hand. 'The gods be praised,' he said.


It took the villagers one week to build a new house. And all this time their fields lay untouched. The women of the village pulled out the stores and cooked food for the many mouths. And when the house was finished it was a fine house – better than before.


Then one night, after the Kumars were settled in their new home and my family sat in a circle on the floor eating our meal, the first rock came through the window. It landed on the cooking pot, knocking the food over the rug.

Bahir rose, ran to the door and flung it open. 'They've gone,' he shouted.

'It's Kamal. We must say nothing,' said Abboo. 'They will soon grow tired.'

'But you can't let them get away with this,' said Bahir. 'I have many friends, we can fight back.'

'Ah, the young. I have lived more years on the earth than you and I have learned that violence will only lead to more violence.' Abboo's voice was calm but sad. 'They will grow tired eventually if we just turn away.'

But they did not grow tired. They took to hanging around our house, threatening us, shouting names, throwing stones, leering at our women, sending threatening letters which made my ammo cry.

'Ignore them,' my father said, angry as he crumpled yet another letter in his hand and threw it onto the fire. 'I will go to the police.'

'Ha! They will not be interested. My friends agree with me.' Bahir paced like a tiger. 'We should teach the gangs a lesson.'

'No.' Abboo stood up. 'You will not fight. There will be no violence from this house.'

'You will let them do this to us? Every night stones in our food. Insults and threats, being pushed and spat on in the street and in the fields, threatening us with what? What is in the letters you hide?'

Abboo shook his head and raised the palm of his hand towards Bahir. 'Pray. That will keep us safe. We must live our lives as usual and hope in time their attention will be turned elsewhere.'

'Listen to your father,' said my mother. 'He is head of the household.' But her face was full of worry and I saw the shadows in her eyes. That day I attended all the prayers of my own will, something I had never done before, and I prayed that we would be safe. Four weeks later, the Kumars packed up their belongings and left in the night.

And still, we silently suffered the abuse.

Electricity was scarce in the village. Abboo had erected pylons bringing power for our house only, but the neighbours brought leads and plugged into our source. Often the demand was too great and the electricity failed.

Ammo was preparing food when the light flickered, dimmed and died. Abboo and Bahir were still at work.

'Electricity dead again,' she cried. 'What can I do? It is a bad thing for a woman to have no food ready for her men to come home to.' She flung up her hands. 'Here, Abdul, you must run to your father's shop and ask him to buy some kerosene for the lamp.' She bent down and

22

looked into my eyes. 'Run quickly. You must return before dark.'

Happy to escape once more to the outside, I stopped for a moment, looking round for any sign of Kamal and his gang. I ignored them now; their insults and spitting did not hurt, but still they scared me. The track was empty. I ran through the fields towards the village. Now and then I thought I heard footsteps behind me, padding on the hard earth or a rustling in the paddy field. I looked around, but no one was ever there.

Suddenly, a low voice called, 'Saaaa-mir'.

This time I did not stop nor look around. Instead I ran and as I ran the footsteps ran behind me. Fast, heavy, more than one person. I ran until my heart pumped so fast I thought it might explode from my chest until suddenly, from between the mango trees and out of the paddy field in front of me, members of Kamal's gang appeared. I spun to go back the way I had come, but others were close on my heels.

'Look,' said one. 'It is the golden boy. Why are you out alone, golden boy? Did your father not hear our warning?' They began to walk around me, hissing insults.

I said nothing. Tears stung my eyes. I closed my fists so tight my nails dug into the palms of my hand.

Someone kicked my legs from under me. I cried out and fell face-first onto the ground. A knee landed in the middle of my back, a hand on my head, grinding my face into the dust.

Kamal grabbed my shirt pulling me to my feet and punched my cheek and ear. He threw me away from him and someone kicked my legs again. I fell over and lay sobbing on the ground. Once more a booted foot crashed into my side.

'Tell your father that this is a warning,' the first gangster said. 'Things are going to get worse.'

I rubbed my eyes and the dust and grit stung. My face hurt where Kamal had punched me. I rose, my legs shaking, my body bending to ease the pain in my side. The gang walked away, laughing. I heard the roar of the motor cycles they had left hidden among the paddy.

I hobbled to my father's shop.

'Abdul, what is it, what happened?' He came round the counter and knelt before me. 'Who did this?' His eyes blazed.

I sobbed out Kamal's name. The muscles of Abboo's neck stood out. His jaw moved from side to side, his lips pulled back and down. 'Dogs, scum,' he said. He grabbed a stout length of wood from some timber he had for sale. 'Watch my son,' he shouted to his assistant and ran out into the night.

'What's he going to do?' I asked the assistant, fearful now for Abboo's life. I had never seen him in such a rage.

'Something that needs doing,' replied the assistant. He put his hand on my shoulder and joined me at the window. 'I have never seen your father like this. They have pushed him too far.'

Sometime later, Abboo returned and threw the wood in the corner. There were splashes of blood on one end. 'Kamal and his friends will not touch you again.' His voice shook. Beads of sweat rolled from his brow.

'You have done well,' said his assistant. 'Those boys deserve worse.' He was all smiles. But Abboo did not smile in return. 'May Allah forgive me,' he said.

I slipped into my father's arms and felt him tremble against me.

From then on I was nervous about going out. The dark held a terror for me, even the daylight hours closed in.

Our Imam agreed to tutor me at home, but what little concentration I had evaporated. I could not learn and the tutor despaired. 'You are nine years old and you cannot read. What is your father paying me to do?'

I only wanted to watch television all day long. I remembered the gang and feared what else they might do.

My fears were not unfounded.

The letters that made my ammo cry and my abboo cover his face in despair arrived almost daily. Mud and stones were thrown at the house. I could not sleep and often wet the bed.

'You must not be afraid,' said Ammo stroking my head, 'Abboo and I will take turns at keeping watch all night. You will be safe.'

Then, one evening, they returned.

They did not come in the dead of night as feared, but when the family was gathered around talking and A'isha and Ammo was serving our evening meal.

In another room I unrolled my bed and brushed away a small insect that ran from the folds. Outside I heard the noises of the early evening; the crickets and the tree frogs and the palm leaves brushing against each other in the breeze. For no reason, the hairs on my neck prickled and I listened more intently. I thought I heard footsteps across the yard, then silence. From the window I could see nothing but normal shapes, black against the moonlight. Fear made my heart beat faster and my head ache. I ran to where the family were gathered.

'Sit down, Abdul,' said Abboo. 'We are about to eat.'

'I think I heard...'

Suddenly the door burst open. Five men in masks with lengths of rope and wooden clubs rushed in. Before Abboo could rise, three were on him. Another two grabbed my brother. A'isha and I huddled in a corner, arms wrapped around each other. My breath stiffened in my chest and I thought I would die from lack of air.

My father was strong and even three men were unable to hold him down. Ammo screeched and lifted the cooking pot. As she rose, one of the gang smashed his club into Abboo's head, knocking him unconscious. Ammo flung the heavy pot full of curry at his assailant. He screamed as the burning liquid sank through his mask and he ripped it from his face. Kamal's eyes met mine and I shrank closer to A'isha. Her body trembled as sobs tore through her.

Bahir spat and cursed, but they had already overpowered him. Kamal hit him in the mouth with his club. 'Gag him', he ordered his men. They tied Bahir's hands and legs and wrapped a gag around his mouth then did the same to Abboo who was beginning to gain consciousness. My mother tried to reach the door, but one of the gang grabbed her and threw her to the ground.

'Don't hurt her,' cried A'isha through her sobs.

The gangster turned his eyes on A'isha. The outline of his mouth betrayed a grin through the mask. He tied my mother up then came towards us, his black eyes never leaving A'isha's face.

Kamal grabbed the guy who was leering at my sister and yanked him backwards. 'I'll deal with them,' he said with a sneer. We could do nothing as he pulled us apart and tied our hands and feet.

Then they stole everything in the house. And they stole my lifeline – the television.

After they had gone, the only sounds were the weeping of the women and moans from my father whose blood spread beneath his face and soaked into the carpet.

It seemed like hours, but it could only have been ten minutes or so before the door opened and the servant girl crept in. Her face was blotched and her eyes swollen. 'I was afraid,' she whispered. 'I hid.'

She undid my mother first and together they released us all.

'You see,' shouted Bahir, after tearing the gag from his already swollen mouth and spitting out the blood. 'Now will you let me find them?'

'No,' said Abboo. 'I was wrong to beat them. You see how violence breeds? If you chase them it will get worse. Tonight might be an end to it.'

Things were quiet for a week or so, but my fear of leaving the house was greater, and with no television, I became sadder and more nervous. I would spend hours staring through the window at the blue of the sky, allowing the soft breeze to cool my skin. Only my time with A'isha brought me any respite from my loneliness. She would read to me and hold me close. Every noise startled me, every rustle in the long grass.

'It's over,' my father told me with sorrow in his eyes. 'You must not be afraid anymore.'

But Kamal's face still haunted my dreams and woke me sobbing in the night; the black hatred in his eyes as he tore the mask from his face told me it was not over.

It was about then my father's younger brother came for a visit. My uncle was a bitter and angry man who had always been jealous of Abboo. His laziness had led his family to the point of starvation. My father had taken him to work with him once, but my uncle wanted payment for doing nothing and Abboo had grown weary of supporting him. Yet he still came, always demanding money, making accusations that my father had cheated him. In our culture it is hard for a man to stomach a brother who is more popular, wealthier and more influential than he is.

'Hello Brother,' Abboo said. They hugged each other. 'I hope you have not come for more money.'

'Not this time.'

Then you have come for a visit – to see how Abdul is perhaps? Come and have food with us.'

My uncle took a seat and Jasmine handed him a plate. He folded a piece of nan bread over and scooped up the curry. After he'd pushed the food into his mouth and chewed for a few minutes, he swallowed and spoke. 'As you know I am poor. You are my brother and I need you to help me.' Although he was younger than Abboo he looked older and his eyes, small and glittery, sank into pockets of flesh.

'Haven't I always helped you?' said Abboo. 'It does no good. Always you want more.'

'How do you help me? A few taka here, a few taka there. This will not help me to become a rich man. You have land you do not need. If you gave it to me, I would use it – make money – be rich like you.'

'My brother, now you ask too much. I work hard for all I have and I need the land for my timber yard. I have plans to expand.'

'Expand? Expand? But I am your brother. You should help me. You would see me wallow in the dust while you help Hindus?'

'I do help you. But I will not give you my land. Even if I did you would not do anything useful. I have offered you employment, but you will not work for me.'

'Why should I work for you? Am I not your equal? We began life as equals, but you take everything.'

All night they argued back and forth. Finally my uncle rose. 'I will not forget this. You are no brother of mine. I could help you – protect you from the gangs – but now things will get worse.'

Abboo pulled himself to his feet. 'Do not threaten me, brother. I do what is right.'

'Then may Allah save you.' His eyes slid to me. 'And the favoured child.'

After that, my father no longer encouraged me to go out. 'I thought there was an end to it,' he said, shaking his head. 'But there will be no end. Now your uncle hates us too and he is a vengeful man.'

One morning, an hour after he had left for work, my father returned home. Ammo saw him come into the yard and she ran to meet him. As I watched he shook his head and put his hands to his face.

'The shop has been ransacked. Everything stolen. Our livelihood. I have to start again.'

Ammo cried out and sank to her knees. 'I cannot bear much more. Surely they will be satisfied now.'

'I am not sure that Kamal is responsible this time,' Abboo said. 'But, my family, we have many friends in this village. Together we will build everything up again.' He held out his hands, calloused with broken nails. 'See these? Rich men pay well for the crafts these hands produce. As long as I have these, we will not starve.' Then he, too, began to cry.

I trembled, but I believed in him. My Abboo was a good man, a brave man, and he had right on his side.

The following day, a woman, Anika Badour, who had married a British-Bangladeshi, came for a visit before she returned to London. My father was the most important man in the village and it was customary for an exile to talk with him before leaving. She was welcomed into our home and given food and water. My parents had many questions about her life in London and she was eager to talk. When it was time for her to leave, she took Abboo to one side. 'I am doing well, but you, brother, I hear you have trouble.'

'Come, we must talk.' He beckoned to my mother. Together they left the house and walked into the yard. I saw their mouths move; heard the raised and lowered voices. Once I heard my name and the word *danger*, but I could not make out all they said.

When they returned, my parents had solemn eyes. I felt a quaking in my spine and I did not know why.

That night my parents sat up late. From behind the closed door, I heard the murmur of their voices and sometimes there were tears in their words. I fell asleep to the music of their hushed conversation.

# Chapter 4

Then one day my tutor did not come. Instead Bahir borrowed a bicycle from a neighbour. 'We are going to Dhaka,' he said. 'For a day out. You are tired of staying in the house I think. We will get your photo taken.'

Indeed the walls of the house had been closing in on me and the blue of the sky and the shouts of my friends from outside had beckoned to me, yet a thousand crawling insects attacked the insides of my stomach whenever I reached the threshold of our home. Somewhere out there was Kamal and his gang and whatever Abboo said, the memory of that night still made me want to throw up. But I would be safe in Dhaka. And I had never had my photo taken. I slipped my hand into Bahir's and clung tightly as we stepped into the morning air. Abboo and Ammo walked behind me and waited as I climbed onto the saddle of the bicycle.

'You will be fine, son,' said Abboo. Ammo wiped her eyes on a fold of her sari and cupped my cheek in her hand.

Bahir seemed in high spirits and he chattered, but his eyes were sad and his mouth moved up and then down as if he was forcing the merriness there.

'Come, it will be a fine day,' he said.

I wrapped my arms around his waist and glanced behind. Even my strong, big brother would be no match for Kamal and his gang.

'Bahir, Abdul, it is good to see you,' shouted a farmer who was driving his slow-moving train of cattle along the track.

Bahir greeted him, but my throat was dry and I could not utter a word.

I looked back at our house. My family stood there, watching us leave and there was something desolate in the way they hung together. As the village faded and grew small in the distance, I settled and began to enjoy the touch of the wind and sun. 'Will we be gone long?' I asked.

'It will be like a holiday.'

Bahir stood on the pedals and we sped along the path through the patchwork fields; the pale lime green of the young paddy, those with established roots, darker and stronger; and fully-mature, the pale-toned, ready to be harvested. We sped beyond the mango trees and onto the main road where the traffic raced by us so quickly I feared for our safety, and to either side, the paddy, the yellow mustard fields and the chilli fields stretched like a canvas of dusty colour.

For many miles we cycled, past Bazar, past other villages and other farms like our own until my hips were sore and my legs were numb from dangling. When we came to a big city with tall buildings and glass fronted shops with western clothes in the windows, we cycled to the railway station where we were met by a friend of Bahir's who took the bike.

Never had I seen such a large station or so many people clogged together in a thick blur. Never had I seen such a train. It seemed to me to be a living thing; a train that went on as far as the eye could see and appeared to be made up of bodies. When it stopped, I realised the bodies were clinging to the sides and roof of the carriages. People rode on the outside of the carriages which came into Bazar, but nothing like this.

'Will we have to do that?' I asked, as the masses leapt from the train and others took their place.

'No, I've booked a seat,' said Bahir, guiding me through the pushing crowds.

It was exciting, riding in the train, watching the countryside slip past and it was good to be away from the house, yet I could not understand why I felt so anxious.

Hours later we rode along the streets of Dhaka in a taxi. The vehicle twisted in and out between the rickshaws, through the surging mass of bodies, past the stores with clothing hanging under the rusted, corrugated roofs and brightly coloured canopies, past tall white buildings and glass fronted shops, cafes and restaurants. Everywhere the noise of the streets surrounded us; the chatter and shouts of voices, the honking of car horns, the swish of bicycle wheels, the creak of the rickshaws. We left the taxi and walked through markets wrapped in the smells of spices, raw flesh, ripe fruit and old clothes. Then we left the streets for crowded alleys flanked by high modern buildings made of concrete blocks and glass.

'This is the house where my friends live,' Bahir said, 'You remember Rohan, who used to live in our village?'

I shook my head. Many people from our village had moved away. I had no memory of them.

'He is a doctor now and his wife is a lawyer. They have a nice house – you will see.'

A security guard in a uniform met us at the door. 'We have come to see Rohan Shah,' said Bahir.

'One minute.' The guard took a telephone from a box in the wall, turned his back to us and spoke into the receiver. He replaced the phone and indicated that we could enter. 'Flat 28,' he said.

At the door of the flat we were met by a handsome, well-dressed man, grey already at his temples.

'Come in, come in.' Rohan stood aside to allow us to enter. The hall was large and high with a shiny floor of tiles. He took us into a vast room, as big as our whole house, with chairs and a huge television. I marvelled at the luxury of the accommodation, but wondered how he could be happy living among all this concrete, so far from the fields and the rivers.

A young woman dressed in a blue sari came from the other room. She had large eyes and long black hair hanging loose around her shoulders. When she spoke her voice was soft like flowing water. 'I am Priya,' she said. 'Welcome to our home. Are you hungry? I have prepared food.'

'You know,' Rohan said to me as we ate, 'Your father helped me to be what I am today. He paid for me to go to medical school. I am so happy to be able to help him now. You will be safe with us.'

Bahir stayed one night. The next day he took me to one side. 'Abdul, you must stay here. I have to go home; there might be trouble and I must be there to help our parents – you understand?'

'But I don't want you to go.' A sudden fear raced through me. 'Why are you leaving me?'

'Do not worry.' He reached into his pocket and brought out a mobile phone and some money. 'You can use this to call me,' he said. 'But not too often.' An unbidden smile stretched my lips. A mobile phone just for me. No other boy of my age had one. He had his name saved on the phone and he showed me how to call him.

'I will come back for you in a week.'

At first I was happy. The couple were kind and they had the biggest TV I had ever seen and I lost myself in movies. They allowed me to lie in bed as long as I wanted, and it was a real bed, like in the films, not a bed roll. Safe from Kamal and his gang, I no longer cowered in a corner. But as time went by and my brother did not return, I began to worry.

Finally I telephoned.

At first he was silent and my worry grew like a snake that twisted in my gut. 'You can't come home. It's not safe for you here. Kamal and his gang have sworn to kill you, the youngest child, and they will lose face if they don't. Worse still, our uncle has turned against Abboo and sided with Kamal. You are going to London. A friend of mine will come and get you.'

'Where is London?'

'It's in another country. The woman who came to visit, Mrs Badour, she is your aunt.' In our culture every woman is aunt and every man is uncle. If they are the same age as yourself, they are brother or sister. It is the way we see each other.

'She lives there in a grand house with big gardens,' he continued. 'She will take good care of you and send you to school.'

'I want to come home.'

'You cannot come home. The danger is too great.'

Tears squeezed from behind my eyes and I could not talk. I sniffed and choked on a sob. A longing to see someone I knew had taken me over. 'Why can't you come to London too?' I spoke at last.

'It's impossible right now. Maybe someday. But Mrs Badour will take care of you. You will be loved and you will be able to play cricket all day. You know, in England they invented cricket.'

He continued to tell me about London, how the people had white skin and lived like kings. How I would be educated and get a good job and marry well when the time came. Above all, I would be safe. And I thought of my new aunt. She had smiled at me as she stroked my head. All the women I had ever met had been kind, why would I think back then that she would prove to be different?

'Will I come home again?' I asked.

'Of course. Abboo will arrange for you to come home as soon as the danger has passed. My friend Taqin, you remember Taqin? He came to visit last time he returned to our village.'

I vaguely remembered the young man in the posh clothes who had gone to school with Bahir and now boasted about how well he had done in the city. I had not liked him much.

'He will take you to have your photo taken and stay with you until we have made the arrangements,' said Bahir. 'Then we will all come to say goodbye.'

Later that night, Taqin arrived to collect me. He was well dressed, his hair slicked back and smelling of limes and coconut oil and when he smiled I caught a glint of a gold tooth.

'You will take good care of this young man,' said Rohan.

'Of course. He is going to have a great life. Tonight I'll take him to a five star hotel, the best in Dhaka – a special treat.' Taqin placed a hand on my shoulder and something in his touch made me shiver.

'We will miss you,' Priya said, and stroked my cheek with the back of her hand.

My heart beat a little bit faster at the thought of leaving this safe place, but Bahir had told me I was going towards a wonderful life and I clung on to that. Maybe I could even learn to play cricket like a professional.

The monsoons had started and the rain cascaded from the sky without pity. Walking was difficult due to the overflowing drains and by the time we reached Taqin's car, my feet and lower legs were wet and dirty. The hotel was a short drive away and it was indeed very grand. Once in the room, Taqin made me wear glasses and a new jacket and he took my photo. 'Now we must wait for your passport,' he said.

I was nervous, but also excited. I was going to London in a country called England! I was going to fly on an aeroplane! I fingered the phone in my pocket, my link to my family whenever I needed them. But I wished I could see my mother and father now. I wanted A'isha to wash and dress me. As I snuggled in my bed, missing my family became almost too much to bear and tears welled up from my heart so that I could not stifle the sobs.

The bed dipped and Taqin climbed in beside me. When he put his arm around me I thought it was for comfort, but he began to rub his hands all over me and to touch me in my private parts. Frightened, I struggled against him but he held me tight and I screamed.

'Shut up,' he shouted and slapped me. I fought him and jumped from the bed. I grabbed my phone, ran to the bathroom and locked the door.

'I didn't touch you!' said Taqin. 'If you tell your brother, I will kill you.'

'I don't care,' I shouted back. I phoned Bahir and when I heard his voice I stammered out what had happened.

For a time there was silence at the other end of the line. When his voice came it was low and cold. 'Just stay there,' he said. 'Don't unlock the door. I am coming to get you.'

All night I lay on the toilet floor. Taqin knocked and knocked. Sometimes he pleaded, sometimes he was angry. I pressed myself against the wall, praying that Bahir would not take too long. Finally, I heard a banging at the door of the room and Bahir's voice. 'Open up,' he shouted. 'If not I will knock the door down.'

'I did nothing,' said Taqin. 'He's lying.' I heard thuds and the door opened.

'I'll kill you,' shouted Bahir.

'Let me explain...' Taqin screamed; his voice trailed away into a gurgle. I crept from the bathroom. Bahir had Taqin around the throat with one hand; the other was a fist that shot forward striking him on the face again and again until blood spouted from his nose. From somewhere Taqin drew a knife. I yelled for help, but no one came. No one would come. Bahir grabbed Taqin's wrist, but not before the blade had sliced his shoulder. And then his

37

blood was mingled with Taqin's and together they crashed into the furniture knocking things over. They landed on the bed and on the floor. Now Taqin was poised above my brother holding him down, one hand reaching for the knife which had flown from his grasp at some stage. With all of my courage, I kicked the knife away. For a moment Taqin looked at me with his eyes full of blackness and hate.

I turned and ran. Out of the room. Down the stairs. Past the hotel staff who stood twisting their hands. Into the streets where the floods flowed like a river.

I ran blindly through relentless rain; rain that filled my eyes, my ears, my nose. The water was up to my knees in places, dragging at my legs, fighting against me. There was no one to help. Bicycles and rickshaws swerved to avoid me, their wheels splashing me until I was soaked through. With my heart thundering in my chest, my head, my ears, I could do nothing but run and run until my breathing hurt my lungs and my legs were too weak to move. I dragged myself up a narrow alleyway where the water swirled down a grater and, with the last of my strength, I collapsed on the raised pavement, just above the water level.

For what seemed like an age, I lay there, until each painful breath eased into something more normal.

'You are running away, I think,' said a voice. I started and lifted my head. An old man I had not noticed before was sitting in the shelter of a corrugated iron lean-to. His clothes were in rags, his feet bare, his beard long and very white. He wore some sort of scarf wrapped around his head. His hair flowed over his shoulders. 'Come,' he said. 'Come into the shelter. All this rain will make you ill.'

I crawled in beside him.

'I know why you are running.' He took my hand and helped me to sit. 'You are afraid.' The brilliant glow of his eyes bore into mine and the unusual colour of them surprised me. They were blue. 'Have you got a taka for an old man?'

I rummaged in my pocket and handed him a taka.

'Thank you. Now I can buy a cup of tea when the tea-boy comes by.' His eyes crinkled and I saw great kindness there.

'Running away solves nothing. Your problem will still be there when you go back. You should fight through it,' he said.

As we sat there, sheltering from the deluge, I told him what had happened at the hotel.

'Why do your family want you to go to England?' he asked.

I told him everything I knew. He nodded and tilted my face up towards him with one hand. His skin was rough and dry. He looked deeply into my eyes for a long time. 'You have to go for a reason,' he said at last. 'You're life will not be easy. Go to England – it is your fate. Fate is like a piece of string, you can change the shape, pull it straight, bend it to your will, but in the end it comes round in a loop. What must happen will happen.'

'But will I come back?' I could not bear never seeing my family again.

'You will come back. You will be happy but sad at the same time. But do not try to change the future.'

I stared at the water rushing past, trying to make sense of what he said. Coke cans, papers, wrappings, all kinds of debris swirled in the water and disappeared down the drain. Suddenly, among the rubble, I saw a five taka note. 'Look,' I shouted, stretching forward, closing my fingers on the note seconds before it reached the drain. 'Five taka.' Triumphant, I turned to my new friend and my breath froze. The space where he had sat was empty. My eyes searched the alley but there was no one lumbering through the ever-deepening water. In the other direction there were only walls – no way out. All that was in the alley was walls – no doors. I pressed my back against the stone, shivering, thinking that something very strange had just happened.

I kept that five taka note for many years until my wallet was stolen in England.

*Go back. What must happen will happen*, the old man had said. I rose slowly and walked through the surging water, back to the hotel, not knowing whether my brother was alive or dead.

I found him on the steps of the hotel. He had removed his shirt and had bunched it up and was now pressing the pad against his shoulder. The rain had washed the blood into pink streaks down his body.

'Where were you?' he asked.

I could not speak, but flung myself on him hugging him close until my sobs became hiccups and I gained control. He picked me up in his good arm. 'I'm taking you home,' he said. 'We will find a way to keep you safe.'

# Chapter 5

Back home my parents cried and hugged me. It was good to be on my own bed-roll, beneath my own mosquito net, being waited on by A'isha.

'I don't want to go to London,' I told my father.

'We will keep you with us if it is possible,' he said. Then he stared at the wall and his voice became strong. 'We will make it possible.'

That night I had a dream about the old man. He appeared before me as if in a glowing light, his beard and hair as white as bleached bone, his eyes blue fire, his lips as red as blood. 'Do not try to change your fate,' he said, and his voice was hollow and came from a distance. I tried to speak, to ask what I must do, but he just smiled and vanished. The next day I remembered the dream vividly and felt that I had done something wrong, but I did not know what. It was just a dream I told myself, but the image stayed with me for a long time.

One night my father and I walked home through the paddy fields in the hour when the sun was low. As it sank from sight, it turned the horizon into a ribbon of red leaving only the blush of a dying day. The mosquitos feasted on our flesh and the cry of the mynah bird was replaced by endless chattering of the tree frogs and crickets, and soon the call to prayer would sound across the land. As the darkness descended and became absolute, leaving only the light of half a moon, I noticed the glow of a cigarette end beneath a mango tree. I stopped and grabbed Abboo's arm. My mouth opened in warning but before I could utter a word, they came.

Jumping from the trees.

Creeping out of the paddy field.

Waving long knives and sticks, their faces masked.

They surrounded us.

The scream stuck in my throat as they wrestled my father to the ground and strong arms lifted me and flung me backwards. Thuds as their feet and sticks rained against Abboo filled my ears. All I could think of was that they were killing him. They were swinging their knives at him and I saw his blood. A wild heat filled my head and I ran at them, kicking, punching, biting.

I was thrown backward.

A fist hit my face.

A foot hit my stomach.

A heavy boot stamped down on my fingers. I heard the snap of bone. Then someone kicked me in the neck.

'Finish it.' A voice rose above the shouting. The one who seemed to be the leader pushed the man who was crouched over me to one side. He laid the sharp edge of his knife against my neck then swung the weapon above his head and he smiled. The long blade glinted in the sparse moonlight.

Time slowed down.

I had a glimpse of Abboo, lying still as his blood spread like a rose around his head.

I squeezed my eyes shut and waited.

I heard the evil laugh.

I felt a thud against my leg and then my chest and thought someone had punched me. I looked down and saw the blood ooze slowly from around the blade. Only then did the pain strike.

The world dissolved.

I woke up to a white light in my eyes. 'Abdul, Abdul, can you hear me?' The face above me was blurred and then gradually became clearer. 'I am Doctor Yonus.'

'Abboo,' I cried, and my voice came out as a hoarse squeak. I tried to move but my body was full of pain.

'Your father is here too. But you must lie still. You have lost a lot of blood.' I was vaguely aware of my family around me murmuring prayers, of the flies crawling over the wall, of the peeling paint above my head.

The doctor switched off the bright light and stuck a needle into my arm and I drifted away. When I came to myself again, Bahir was leaning over me. 'We're taking you to hospital in Dhaka,' he said. 'Our friend, Rohan, with whom you stayed, he is arranging it for me.'

Without the strength to form the words, I tried to ask about Abboo again.

'Hush now,' said Bahir. 'Save your strength.'

Slipping in and out of consciousness, I was carried to a car and laid in the back seat. I knew no more until I woke up in a white room and wondered whether I was in paradise; a featureless white room where angels drifted around me praying for my recovery in soft voices.

Next thing I remember was waking up with Doctor Rohan leaning over me. 'How are you?' he asked.

I parted parched lips but could not speak. Above me the walls were white and clean. I slipped away again.

The weeks passed and I gradually regained my strength, each period of clarity lasting longer. Figures moved around the room chanting prayers and I eventually I came to realise that the angels of my dreams were earthbound; my friends and family.

Nurses with soft hands took care of me, feeding me and sponging my body and tending to all my needs while I suffered the cycle of travelling from this world to a place of dark pain, then to a place where there was no pain at all and back to the world again. I lost all track of time.

Then one night, I opened my eyes and the old man was standing by my bed with his red lips and his blue, blue eyes, looking down at me from what I felt was a great height. 'I told you not to change things,' he said.

'What did I change?' I asked.

'You tried to change your fate.' He held up a stick. It was smooth and amber and shone. 'This is *my* life. See how straight it is?'

'Who are you?' I whispered.

'I have come to tell you that it is your fate to help others. You must go with the stream. Do not try to take a different path.'

'What do you mean?' I said. But he just smiled. 'When the bad dreams come, chant the words you learned in the mosque. That will calm you.' He touched my head. His hand was cool and firm and he smelt of rose-water and cinnamon.

With his touch, my body jolted as if I had been suddenly awakened from a deep sleep. Had I been asleep? I hadn't thought so. The lights, the hospital ward, the noises of shoes against tiled floors, the click of instruments and the bleep of the machine attached by wires to my chest, all came into focus. There was a figure by the bed and for a second I thought... but the mist cleared and it was Doctor Rohan.

He was staring at me, his head a little to one side. 'Who were you talking to?' he asked.

'I was ... dreaming.'

He pressed his fingers against my wrist and looked at his watch. 'Don't worry. Because of the trauma, you will have many dreams. Try to sleep.'

But I could not sleep again that night.

Then my Abboo came to visit. He was using a crutch and had a bandage around his head and neck. He didn't speak, just sat by my bed and held my hand, tears running down his cheeks. I was so happy that he'd survived the attack, I wanted to hug him, but had no strength to raise myself.

I told him about the old man, how he had disappeared in the alleyway, how he came back in dreams, how he had appeared beside my bed. Abboo looked at me with troubled eyes.

The next time Doctor Rohan came to see me he said, 'I have talked with your family. As I have explained, you have had a very bad experience. Healing will take time; your mind as well as your body. You may have strange dreams for the rest of your life.'

Most of the dreams were bad. Nightmares in which I was walking along the track through the paddy fields. The rice stalks were an impossible golden yellow. Overhead the mango trees stretched their branches across my path, black and ominous against the glare of the paddy, their leaves larger than life and a deep blue. Wanting to turn and run, but compelled to move forward, I walked towards them. Suddenly shadowy figures leapt from the trees. They had long sharp finger-nails, glowing eyes and mouths that dripped blood. They swarmed all over me and I could hear their laughter. I would wake up, weak and sweating, fighting with my blanket. In spite of the explanations from the doctor, my family believed I was possessed by a devil.

Once we were both out of hospital, my father sent a private car to the city for the head spiritual leader, the High Imam. As well as being a very holy man, the High Imam is what people in the west would call a spiritual healer. His prayers had the power to lift evil and to cure minds and bodies.

The High Imam was a striking figure dressed in flowing white robes, his beard, white and full, his deep brown eyes shining with a pure light. In his hand he carried a string of beads. There was a stillness about his face and he brought with him an aura of calm and the air around him smelt fresh and clean with a hint of sweet roses, vanilla and lime. My first impression was how clean he appeared. Even the dust outside did not cling to his sandalled feet. As he entered the house, everyone fell silent. I immediately knew I was in the presence of someone very special.

We spoke alone for several hours. I told him in detail everything that had happened and what was still happening to me. Listening intently, he nodded his head from time to time. Just being in his company filled me confidence and peace.

I asked about the old man. 'Who was he?'

'It could be your grandfather,' the Imam said. 'Because you are so young, he will come as an angel to guide you. This is nothing bad. You have no devils. I have prepared holy water, here drink.' He offered me a vial. 'Your father must make a gift of a cow to the poor and they will pray for you.' He gave my ammo a locket to give to me. 'This will protect him from harm,' he said.

After his ritual, he left to speak to my parents. He told us that everything would be fine now and we would not need him again. Before leaving, he accepted a bag of rice and his fee.

# Chapter 6

Family life was more relaxed after that. I went to the mosque for lessons and was waited on by my sister and guarded by my brother and I believed that the High Imam's words were true – that this locket and his blessing would keep me safe.

But several days later everything changed again.

After prayer, when the family gathered together to eat, Jasmine came running in. 'The High Imam has come back. He is looking for Abdul.'

My father went to meet him. 'What is the matter? You have come from so far? What is wrong with my son? What is it? You could have sent someone else – this must be serious.'

The Imam raised his hand. 'Please, please calm down. I have to see Abdul now.'

This time he was nervous, his normally placid face drawn and his eyes full of fear. Beads of sweat ran down his cheeks as he spoke to me. Once again he wanted me to tell him everything from the beginning. This time when he listened he was tense and did not nod. Then he sighed deeply. 'This is not easy. You are very special boy. Think about things very carefully; do what you have to do, not what you want to do.'

Confused by his words, I asked, 'What do you mean? I don't know what to do. I don't know what I want to do.'

'That is the problem. That is what you have to find out.'

He steepled his fingers and studied the ceiling. 'Sometimes we have to travel,' he said.

'But what am I meant to do?' I asked, fear tightening my belly and throat. 'I don't know what to do.' I couldn't understand his words.

'Close your eyes and follow your heart. Always be true to yourself. Your life will not be easy.'

I watched him leave the room. I had no idea what he meant and the good feelings he left me with before had gone.

I closed my eyes, but my heart told me nothing.

My mother clasped her hands before the Imam. 'What is it? What's wrong?' she said, but he waved her away. 'I must spend the night in prayer,' he said. 'You must provide me with a room.'

'Of course,' said my father immediately, and gave orders to have a room thoroughly cleansed so that the High Imam could have privacy.

The next morning, he had gone.

Abboo shook his head. 'There must be something wrong. He came all this way and left without payment.'

'I will go to him and pay him for his time and if I can find out more, I will,' said Bahir.

My brother went to the city and to the high mosque to find the Imam, but no one there had seen him for days. We were never able to contact him again.

The following day after my brother's return, when the sun was high, my father took me for a walk. We sat in the shade beneath the mango tree. Everything was quiet in the midday heat. Even the ants had retreated underground.

Abboo gave me a mango to eat. 'It is up to you,' he said. 'If you stay here I will do my best. You will have land and family, but you will always be in danger and you will not have an education. If you leave, it will be best for you. Kamal will not stop until you are dead.'

'I want to stay here,' I said, then I remembered the Imam's words. *Do what you have to do, not what you want.* And that made me afraid.

'There will be better chances for you in England. You will be safe there. You can come home every year and we'll meet you in Dhaka. I will send you ticket money. I don't want you to go, but remember what happened – next time it will be worse. You are very dear to me – to us all and I worry for your life.' His voice trembled on the last few words.

'Can't we all go?' I said.

'Ah, if only it were possible.' He shook his head.

'If that's what I have to do.' My voice was small.

'I will write to Mrs Badour tonight,' he said, and silently we studied the horizon where the air flickered and shimmered in a white heat and I shrank into the shade as a snail shrinks from the sun.

That night the nightmares returned.

# Chapter 7

About a month later, a woman came to the house and said she was a sister of Mrs Badour and was going to take me to London to live with my aunt. Her name was Mrs Din, she said. During our meal she told us what a wonderful life I was going to have. Her smile appeared kind, but her eyes were hard and frightened and they fastened on my face in a way I did not like.

Every time I closed my lids in sleep, the nightmares waited to assault me – sometimes vague, always frightening. That night, the dream changed. I saw myself in England in a dirty, dark room and I was being beaten, kicked, punched and finally stabbed in the leg. I tried to scream, but only silence came from my open mouth. And then there was blood, pouring from my leg, pouring down the walls. The steady beat of my heart grew louder until it filled my head and I was choking and vomiting between my gasps and screams. As I struggled for wakefulness, the horror went and I was in a field with a gentle breeze and sunlight warm on my skin and a feeling of peace came over me. I saw myself running over green grass, and kids swinging flat bars of what looked like wood on chains. Then the dream changed again and I was in a room wearing a suit and a couple of smartly dressed girls with white skin and fair hair came in. One smiled at me and my eyes followed her. I reached out to take something from her hand and she dissolved before I touched her. I had never seen a white person at that time. Suddenly I was back in my bedroom and the old man was sitting in a chair, his face bright with approval. 'Don't forget who you are,' he said. 'What is meant to happen will happen.'

Only then did I become fully awake and the room was empty, with flies buzzing around outside my net and my ammo's voice scolding someone in the kitchen. I clearly remember the details of that dream till this day.

The images in the dream would not leave me and filled my head until the need to spill them out overcame me. Throughout the early meal I related every detail to my family, trembling as each memory hit me with a new force.

My brother looked at me with disbelieving eyes, while Abboo tried to explain the dream away. 'It is only the worry of going to a strange land,' he said. 'I told you about people with white skin and your mind has conjured them up. I'm sure you will be well looked after in England. If this were not the case, I would not send you.'

My father was wise and I believed him. Nevertheless, I was troubled and could not eat. That morning I prayed with my family and trusted my life and my fate to Allah.

Afterwards, in the quiet of the morning, I sat in the doorway with my possessions in a holdall by my side. I still had the five taka note that I had found in Dhaka tucked in a wallet given to me by brother. The birds sang in an empty sky and the voices of the workers calling to each other reached me from the fields. Above me the palms trees towered, their whispering fronds gently waving, throwing sun patterns on to the dust below. The flies settling on my face and arms barely troubled me, my stomach was in so many knots. From the distance the low hum of a motor grew and I watched the hire car materialise from a cloud of dust between the paddy fields. Mrs Din had arrived to collect me.

The wheels ground to a halt. The door opened and Mrs Din stepped out wearing a deep purple sari with yellow edges. I rose to my feet and she held out a hand, her bracelets jangling, her nails long, like talons.

My family hugged me and cried. They had grouped together with all my friends and neighbours to wish me luck. I tried to hold back the tears, to be brave, but it was too much. I did not want to leave my family again and clung to them in turn, absorbing their warmth. I clung most of all to my father.

'You still have your phone to call us,' said Bahir with his hand on my head. 'You will return a rich man.'

'Come, we must go now,' Mrs Din said impatiently. 'The driver is waiting.' The car engine idled in the morning air. A mynah bird called from the distance. A cockerel crowed. The sun dappled on my face, its rays filtered by the palm leaves.

My abboo bent down and put his hands on my shoulders. 'I have given money to your aunt for your keep and education and promised her the stretch of land beside my shop. If there's anything you need, ask her. Anything. I will send more money when needed.' He hugged me again, so tightly I couldn't breathe. Finally he let me go and his cheeks were wet. 'You will come home for a few weeks every year. I have money set aside for your fare. Time will soon go by, you'll see.'

Ammo placed the locket around my neck. 'Keep this always, my son. It will guide you safely back to us one day.'

My feet were heavy and moved slowly. My heart hammered like to burst free from my chest. I studied the ground before me until I climbed into the back of the car and then I watched that small group of people through a mist of tears; my family and friends, standing in a huddle, waving and waving until they grew small in the distance.

Mrs Din punched numbers on her phone. 'We've left,' I heard her say. 'I'll phone you again when we get near the airport.'

I don't recall much more of that journey. My heart fluttered. That day I left home, and I never truly returned.

Several hours later Mrs Din phoned someone again. 'We are approaching the airport.' And she gave the registration number of the car. 'Yes, you'll be there? Yes.'

When the car drew to a stop, a policeman walked over and peered through the window. His face was lean and hard, his eyes black like night and I shrank into my seat. Police scared me. He opened the door and smiled, showing smoke-stained teeth.

'Come on,' snapped Mrs Din.' He's a friend.' She brought out a thousand taka note and handed it to the driver.

That seemed like an awfully lot of money. 'You gave him too much,' I said, when he made no effort to give her any change. She did not reply, but a look passed between her and the policeman. She brought a pair of glasses from her pocket and told me to wear them.

'Why?' I asked.

'Just do as you're told,' she snapped.

More out of curiosity than any desire to obey this woman, I put them on; the glass was clear.

'Hurry.' The policeman took my hand. 'I will get you aboard.'

As soon as the driver opened the boot for the luggage, Mrs Din reached in and grabbed a small, red holdall.

'I'll carry that for you,' said the policeman.

'No, no. I'll take it.' She clutched it to her.

The airport was a big, dusty building with hundreds of people milling around and standing in lines. The policeman led us through a large hall where queues of passengers stood before a long desk. There were grumblings and mutterings as we walked past them to the front. Finally someone shouted out, 'Hey, we have been here for hours. You cannot go before us.'

'These are special guests,' replied the policeman, and the mutterings fell silent.

Special? What was so special about me? I decided then that Mrs Din must be more important than we knew and gazed at her with new respect. She handed the man behind the desk the passports. He glanced at them and gave us two long tickets which she tucked inside the passports. 'Our boarding passes,' she told me.

The policeman did not let go of my hand and took us through a door that led directly to the plane. No one stopped to check us for security which surprised me. I had watched many films and I wondered why we were just walking onto the plane; had the films been false? Was there really no security?

The police officer let go of my hand. Mrs Din handed him a package.

'Go ahead, board the plane,' he said, turned and left. The plane was empty except for the cleaners who were just leaving. Mrs Din directed me to a seat, then opened my passport and showed me a photo of myself wearing glasses. She tapped the name with a long fingernail. It was another half hour before the passengers began to board. As the passengers settled in their seats, a man in a smart uniform stood up and began to talk. He pointed out the escape routes and told us what to do if the plane crashed into the sea. Then he took out a yellow life jacket and pulled it over his head. I had never considered the possibility of the plane crashing before.

'Do planes often crash, Auntie?' I asked, concerned.

'I've flown many times quite safely,' she said.

Unconvinced, I shrank into my seat.

The plane jolted and crawled forward. It turned around and with a great roaring noise began to speed up. Clutching the armrests in alarm, I felt myself pressed back into my seat. Once we climbed into the air, I relaxed and the fear slid from me to be replaced by excitement and for a short time, the sorrow of leaving my family was forgotten. I was actually flying. I stared out of the window, amazed at the speed of which the houses and fields and city shrank into miniatures and rivers and mountains spread out below us.

We flew for an age until the pilot told us we would soon be landing in Singapore.

'Where is Singapore, Auntie?' I asked her. 'I thought we were going to London.'

'Be quiet.' Her voice was sharp like needles, her eyes like black rock. 'That bag, the red one I have? When we get off the plane you carry it. Do not let anyone touch it.' She pointed a bony finger at my face. Her bracelets jangled. 'If you do I'll beat you until you die.' The deadly flash in her eyes told me she would be more than capable of carrying out her threat.

As we left the plane and headed for immigration, I asked again. 'Why are we going to Singapore? I thought we were going to London.'

She slapped me – hard. 'Not so many questions. If anyone asks you to open that bag you start to cry.' She raised her hand and I saw the rings glint and felt again the pain where they had scraped my cheek. Gone was the woman who had been nice to me in my father's house; here she looked angry and nervous. The airport in Singapore appeared like a bigger version of the one we had left. She took me to a hotel with wide corridors and a lift.

'I'm thirsty, Auntie,' I said, as she unlocked the door to our room.

'Don't bother me.' She put shaking hands to her face. Her mouth moved as if she was speaking but no sound came.

'But I want a drink,' I said again.

'Get something in there.' She pointed to the mini-bar. At that time I had no idea what it was; it was just a box in the corner. She began to pace, praying in whispers and wringing her hands.

I opened the door of the box. Inside the air was cool and there were bottles and cans. Afraid to disturb her again, I lifted a can which I thought was coke. I pulled out the ring and tipped the can to my lips. Cold, bitter liquid filled my mouth. It tasted nothing like coke. Although I did not like the taste, I drank two more cans before my thirst was quenched. Mrs Din was still pacing and praying. My head began to swim and I fell face down on the bed wondering why I felt so weird, then sleep overcame me.

Next morning I awoke to her shouting and dragging me from the bed. My head was pounding, my stomach heaved and I ran to the toilet and was sick in the bowl. When I returned to the bedroom she was standing with an empty can in her hand, her eyes furious. 'You bad, bad boy,' she screamed. 'Do you know what this is? This is alcohol.' And she slapped me so hard my already fragile head felt as if it would explode. 'You will make us late.'

All I wanted to do was go back to bed. 'I'm ill,' I said.

She slapped me again so that I staggered backwards. I cried out.

'It's what happens when you drink alcohol.' Her voice pierced like arrows in my ears. She pushed me in front of her to the lift and into a room where people were eating. I looked at the food. It was strange and smelt funny and I imagined I would die if I put any of it in my mouth. I struggled not to be sick again.

Fighting the urge to lay my aching head on the table, I stared at my empty plate while Mrs Din helped herself from the breakfast bar. Once her hunger was satisfied, we walked through the terminal to security.

'Remember, no one gets to look in that bag,' she said. 'And wear the glasses.' Then she began to mutter prayers under her breath. This time we took our place in the queue and waited our turn. All the time my head spun and I felt so ill. I wondered why people drank alcohol if this is what it did to them. When we reached the check point, we were stopped.

'Open the bag, please,' said a man in uniform. It was not necessary to pretend to cry; I was missing my family and felt confused and upset, hungry and sick at the same time. Tears came easily.

'That is a kid's bag. It's only school books. He does not like people touching him or his stuff; he is a special child – you know?' said Mrs Din.

The guard stared at me and I felt the weight of his eyes and cried harder. He turned his head to look at Mrs Din who could not stand still. She set a hand on my shoulder and I felt the tremble. 'Why have you come to Singapore when you are going to London?' he asked.

'The only flight we could get.' Her voice wavered.

'That is not true. There are many flights going to London.'

'My mother is dying. I have to get home.' She adjusted her head scarf and cleared her throat. Lifting the edge of her sari sleeve, she dabbed her eyes. 'Please,' she sobbed. 'My mother...'

The guard opened my passport, looked at it and studied me. 'Why does he have a Bangladeshi passport when you have a British one?'

'He is my nephew. I am taking him to see his grandmother before she dies. We could not get a flight at the last minute. This is the only way we can do it.'

She sounded convincing. She covered her face with her hands and sobbed.

I cried harder and clutched the bag to me.

'I'll have to call my superior,' said the guard.

Mrs Din gasped. Each breath shook as she pulled it into her lungs. The guard called another man and explained that I would not let him look in the bag.

'He's a special child. It upsets him,' Mrs Din said, before taking another bout of weeping. Just then the guard's phone rang. He raised his eyebrows at the manager. 'Emergency. Someone's collapsed.'

'Okay, little brother,' said the manager to me. 'We will just put it through the x-ray machine, how about that?' I nodded and sniffed, wiping my nose on the back of my hand. Mrs Din's fingers dug into my flesh like talons.

'There, all done,' said the guard and handed the bag to me. The hand on my shoulder relaxed. I took the bag and wiped my eyes.

Looking back, I must have been a sorry sight. I was shaking, suffering my first hangover, my clothes crumpled, my nose running, but even then I wondered why the guard could not see how nervous Mrs Din was.

As we boarded the plane to Heathrow, she told me not to look at anyone and to keep my head down, otherwise she would beat me.

Silently I thanked Allah that Mrs Badour would soon be picking me up and I could leave this horrible woman.

About an hour into the flight I became bored and fidgeted in my seat. I put my feet up on the seat in front and she slapped me. 'You are a very bad child,' she hissed. 'Will you sit still?' When eyes turned in our direction, she pursed her lips and stared at her hands. At least when they played a movie I had something to focus on. The staff brought strange looking food in plastic dishes, but my stomach was still too upset to taste it.

My first impression of England was the cold. When the aircraft door opened, the wind struck me, the coldest wind I had ever known. It was August in London.

I expected Mrs Badour to be waiting for us, but as I looked around, all I could see was a sea of strangers. If I had been impressed by the airport in Singapore, the sheer size of Heathrow overwhelmed me. Thousands of people milling around. Most of them were white, but there were many more nationalities.

Afraid and nervous as well as excited in this strange new world, I stuck close to Mrs Din, so that I wouldn't lose her. There were moving floors and staircases with people standing on them; the ceiling seemed to be glass, every surface shone back at me. There were cafes and shops, all glittering and clean. Finally we came to a large hall and joined a queue.

'Get out your passport,' ordered Mrs Din. Once again she had become very anxious. 'Don't look at anyone and don't let anyone look in that bag.'

It was difficult to obey. All those faces, so different from what I had been used to. A white man with a shiny, bald head and a moustache stood in a booth in front of our queue looking at passports and asking questions.

When our turn came, the white guy asked me why I was coming to Britain and I told him the story of my grandmother dying. His phone rang and a young woman came and joined him in his booth. Her eyes were blue and they reminded me of the eyes of the old man. I had never seen a woman so pale with pink in her cheeks and such light hair. I could not wrench my eyes away from her face. She raised her eyebrows at the man who was chattering into his phone and he jerked his thumb in the air. The young woman said something in English to Mrs Din and we moved on.

As soon as we had passed through, Mrs Din's demeanour changed. She threw her head back and laughed. 'We did it,' she said. 'We are home.' She snatched the bag from me. She almost danced through the crowds. 'Now we collect our suitcases.'

She took me into another room where there was a long moving belt with luggage on it. While we waited for ours, she took out her phone. 'I'll call your aunt now, tell her we have arrived.' She tapped the buttons.

59

After speaking for a few minutes, her voice rose. The black anger had returned and hung around her like a shroud. It sounded as if they were having an argument. I heard her say, 'I cannot wait.' Then she turned to me. 'Follow me.' She took me to where there were more cafes and shops.

'I'm hungry, Auntie,' I said, as the smell of food made my empty stomach rumble.

'That's your own fault. Sit right here at this table and don't move. Your aunt will come for you soon.' She grabbed the front of my shirt, put her face close to mine and held up the red holdall. 'If you ever tell anyone about this bag, I will see that your mother and father die in their sleep.' Droplets of spittle landed on my face. She pushed me away and turned on her heel, leaving me there.

I couldn't understand what was happening. Nothing added up. If she was Mrs Badour's sister, why was she leaving me alone? Why did *she* not take me to the Badour's house?

For two hours I waited in the terminal. I was hungry, cold, and so dirty I could smell myself. I had not had a wash and had nothing to eat since I left Bangladesh. Nevertheless, the number of people with different coloured skin and strange clothes amazed me and drew my attention away from my predicament. Why did Allah create so many different peoples, I wondered. So many of them, well dressed and rich looking and staring at me as they walked past. Afraid and lonely, I pressed myself into the chair and fought back the tears.

Then I noticed an Asian man with a stick limping around the terminal. His belly hung over the top of his trousers but his shoulders were narrow. One foot pointed away from the other and slapped the ground as he walked. From between pillows of fat, his eyes lit on me and he

60

came over. As he drew near, I could smell spices and curry from his clothes and my stomach rumbled.

'Abdul?' he asked.

All I could do was nod.

'I am Hassan Badour, your uncle.'

Now my tears were of relief. I grabbed my holdall and followed him.

'We're taking an underground train,' he told me, then laughed when he saw my look of surprise. How could a train go under the ground?

'You will see,' he said as if he had read my thoughts. He led me down a flight of steps and into a station with machines that stamped tickets. I pressed close to him as people rushed around us. Everyone was in such a hurry.

'Down the stairs,' he said.

I stepped forward and stopped. Here were more stairs that moved and I was expected to stand on them. I decided then that this country had many lazy natives.

'What is the matter?' said Uncle.

'The stairs are moving.'

He laughed. 'They are meant to. Come, try.'

Tentatively I took a step forward and grasped the rail, giving a cry as it moved also.

'Jump off at the bottom,' Uncle told me.

At first I was nervous, but by the time we had reached the bottom, I realised what fun this was. 'Can we do it again?' I asked. Stopping, I watched another staircase travelling upwards. If I jumped on it, I could go to the top and then down once more.

My uncle snapped his fingers and said, 'At the other side. Then we go up.'

The train arrived, moving smoothly. Clean carriages with no one riding on the outside. Doors slid open. 'Go on, go on,' Uncle pushed me before him. I jumped through the open door and it hissed shut behind us. The carriage was full of people so that we had to stand. Swaying with the movement of the train, I grabbed a shiny pole that reached from floor to ceiling to steady myself.

Once we left the train, I happily jumped on the moving staircase, my mind already running forward to later, when I phoned home. What tales I would have to tell!

As we walked along the street, this strange street with high buildings and beautiful shops and all these people in nice clothes and the smell of food drifting from eating houses, my eyes darted in every direction, committing as much to memory as I could.

Uncle stopped behind a queue. 'Now we take a bus.'

The bus was a double-decker and we rode upstairs. It was nothing like the buses back home, often so full they tilted to one side as the passengers hung onto railings. I had never seen a double-decker before and thought it the most amazing mode of transport yet. My mouth fell open as I looked all around trying to digest everything in this peculiar new place.

'Women drive cars here?' I asked in amazement.

He laughed and his belly shook. 'Of course they do.'

This was indeed a land where I could do well. I was happy I had come for these great opportunities, but my home and family stayed in my mind. I missed them so much already. Then I remembered what the old man had said, 'You will be happy but sad at the same time.' and 'You will return.'

For a while I forgot my hunger; I was overcome by this magical place.

'Did you like Mrs Din?' Uncle's words stabbed my thoughts.

Not wanting to admit that I had been afraid of her, I shrugged my shoulders.

'Did she give you anything to carry?'

Her warning words about killing my parents still rang in my ears. I mumbled that I didn't know anything and stared at my hands.

After we left the bus we walked into what I now know is a council estate with blocks of flats seven floors high. We passed a green field and there, among other strange shaped things, I saw the bar of wood with chains and kids swinging on them. I stopped and grabbed my uncle's arm. 'What is that,' I asked, pointing.

'That's a play park. You can go there with my children.'

'Those things on chains?'

'Swings. What's wrong?'

'Nothing.' I shook my head. I couldn't tell him I had seen those swings and that green field in my dreams.

The flat was five floors up. 'Here we go.' He opened the door. The welcome smell of curry came out to greet me.

'You found him,' said Mrs Badour. 'Come in and meet the others.' She did not smile at me but turned away. My first impression was of a room which seemed to be crowded with people. The Badours had four children. The oldest son's wife Basmah and her three babies also lived there.

'You'll have to sleep on the couch. Set your things there.' My aunt pointed to the wall. Her mouth was sour and she did not look happy.

'Why do I have to sleep on the couch?' I asked.

'You see my family? Where do they all sleep? I have only three bedrooms. Why do you think you should have a bedroom?'

I couldn't believe this. When a visitor comes to Bangladesh, they are accepted immediately. Food and drinks are brought out and they are given the best room for their privacy. Nothing is spared. I had expected a similar welcome, but my new 'aunt' was behaving as if she wished I was not there.

'When you come to Bangladesh you have a room. You told my father you had a nice big house and a car.' I straightened my shoulders and stared at her.

'This is a nice big house,' she said, her voice rising. 'And we do have a car.' She sniffed the air. 'Have a bath. Then I will give you some food.'

'I am hungry. I want food first.'

'Go run him a bath, Rubana,' Aunt said to a girl who was about my age.

'I'm hungry,' I repeated. 'At home I eat when I'm hungry.'

She made a tutting noise, filled a plate with curry and nan bread and thrust it at me. 'You are not at home now. This you had better learn.'

I grabbed the plate. Never had food been eaten so fast.

'I've run your bath,' said Rubana. 'Come.' She was a pretty girl, very slim with large dark eyes and shiny hair in a single braid. She led me to a small room and I stopped at the open door. The air was damp and smelt of flowers. 'You expect me to bathe in that?' I asked, staring in horror at the tub. I had been used to washing in a pond where I could swim and splash. How on earth was I ever going to wash in such a small space?

She looked hurt. 'It's clean and I've put bubbles in for you.'

'There's no room,' I replied. 'I won't fit in there.' Rohan and his wife had had a shower-room, which had seemed strange at the time. There had also been a shower in the room in Singapore, but a tub was new.

My aunt appeared behind her. 'This is a bath. It is how we do it in this country. You think we have a pond in the street? Where you think we have pond? Shut the door, take off your clothes and get in. And when you're finished, wear this.' She handed me a robe and indicated to her daughter to leave. 'Then give me your clothes – I have to wash them.'

I climbed into the tub and, unsure of what I was supposed to do next, remained standing. The water was scented and warm and it did feel good around my legs. I knelt down, slid on the smooth surface and fell forwards landing on my hands and knees. Then my hands slipped and I went face first into the bubbles. The water splashed over the rim. Panicking, I breathed in a mouthful of soapy water and struggled to raise myself. The soap stung my eyes and rubbing them only made them worse.

'Abdul – what are you doing in there?' My uncle opened the door and came fully into the room. 'Do not let your aunt see this mess,' he whispered, his eyes opening wide when he saw the puddle on the floor, but there was laughter in his voice. 'Here, wipe your face.' He handed me a towel.

Coughing and spluttering I struggled into a sitting position.

'Now wash.' He brought a cloth from the basin and offered it to me. 'Rub yourself all over with this.'

Once I'd dried my eyes, he set the towel to one side. 'And afterwards mop up the floor.' Still smirking, he left me alone. I sank into the bubbles. It did feel relaxing, and I washed away the grime of the last forty-eight hours. When I returned to the living room wearing the robe, everyone was sitting at a table eating.

'Here comes Freshy,' said Rubana.

'My name is Abdul.' I was confused.

Everyone laughed.

'You will be called Freshy, because you are fresh from Bangladesh,' Uncle said. After that, I was not known as Abdul in that house.

The journey had been long and this day full of surprises. The flat was small, but every room had light at the turn of a switch, every tap gushed water, hot or cold as you liked. From the window I could see tall buildings, a road with orderly traffic in a steady stream, and the green field with the swings from my dreams.

When my parents phoned that night my heart leapt; it was so good to hear their voices. I had so much to tell them. They laughed at my enthusiasm and when I related my encounter with a bath tub. After the phone call, I was so tired I curled up on the floor, imagining the comfort of the couch, but having to wait for the others to go to bed. I watched television, enjoying the pictures because the programmes were in English, a language of which I had no knowledge. It did not matter anyway, because of the noise in the room; Auntie and Basmah shouted at each other and at the children quarrelling and laughing in turn, babies crying, Uncle scolding, and all in this strange foreign language. My eyes grew heavy and I drifted into sleep where I lay.

In the morning, after prayers, I was given a bowl with milk and small round things floating in it. 'What is this?' I asked.

'Rice Krispies,' said Rubana.

I stared, wondering how I would manage these strange looking rice grains and thought of the spicy puffed rice my ammo made and gave us to eat with our fingers out of twists of paper. Maybe I should drink it. I raised the bowl to my lips.

'What are you doing, Freshy? Use the spoon. What, you've never used a spoon before?' Auntie raised her eyes to the ceiling.

'Yes, I've used a spoon,' I said, embarrassed. I had occasionally used a spoon to eat a rice and vegetable dish, but mostly spoons were used for serving food back home. It is customary in our culture to eat with the fingers, using the nan bread to scoop up curry.

They all watched me in delight as I tried to manoeuvre the spoonful of cereal into my mouth. Rubana laughed most of all.

Uncle and his son then left the house. The son worked long hours in a restaurant and was seldom at home. I do not know what my uncle did. He claimed to be unfit to work, but he left the house most days.

Auntie brought me clean clothes. 'Get dressed and then get out, all of you.'

'Where will I go?' I asked.

'Come to the swing park with us, Freshy,' Rubana said. 'Ammo is in a bad mood in the mornings.'

Although the children could speak Bengali, they were better at English and only resorted to Bengali when they directly addressed me. At first Rubana laughed at my lack of knowledge, called me stupid and, encourage by her, the other kids did the same. But I loved the park, the swings, the slide, the roundabout.

As the day drew to a close, Rubana seemed to like me better and became my champion when the English kids taunted me. By the end of the first week we were firm friends. She taught me English words and how to play football.

I missed my family and I hated sleeping on the couch. The Badours always seemed to be angry, forever shouting at each other. The house was so crowded, that for the first time in my life, I was looking forward to going to school. I listened intently as Rubana and the other kids tried to teach me English, and I enjoyed playing in the park. At first my parents phoned every night and their call was the highlight of my day.

I was still having nightmares of shadowy figures with long nails leaping at me from the trees, but when my uncle asked me why I cried out in the night, I told him only that I had bad dreams. Their son and his wife largely ignored me and seemed to resent my presence.

One night, after everyone except my uncle and aunt was in bed and I was snuggled down on the couch pretending to be asleep, they began to talk about an arranged marriage between myself and Rubana.

I was horrified. I was only ten. I did not want to get married. When my parents phoned I told them what I had heard. 'How do you feel about this girl?' asked Abboo.

'I do not want to marry her,' I said.

'Then do not worry; you have many years yet. You may change your mind.'

After that, being around Rubana embarrassed me, so I stayed away from her.

'Do you want to play on the swings?' she would ask. I continued to ignore her. Knowing I had been expected to marry her made my skin prickle and the words stick in my throat.

She followed me around, hurt in her eyes. 'What's the matter, Abdul? Why are you not my friend anymore?' I turned away, my face hot. Even being in the same room as her now became uncomfortable. I did not know whether she was aware of her parents' plans, but in my mind I believed she must be.

Eventually she gave up and I grew closer to her younger siblings.

One night, the telephone rang and, expecting my parents, I stood by as my aunt answered it, waiting for her to pass it to me.

'We need to talk. We need more money,' she said into the receiver. She listened for a beat. Then her voice rose. 'His education is going to cost a lot more than we thought. He needs a uniform, he needs books and pens. You have to send more money.

'I know how much you gave me, but it's not enough. Things are not good here. Prices rise. He eats so much.'

Then my uncle took the phone from her hand. 'My wife tells the truth. Everything is getting more expensive these days. You want us to do the best for your son, you have to send us more money.'

Then he covered the mouthpiece with his hand. I watched the smile slowly drag the corners of his mouth. 'They're going to send more,' he whispered. And my aunt smiled too. Only then did they pass the phone to me.

After that my uncle and aunt had a serious conversation in English.

# Chapter 8

As time went on, my aunt's dislike of me intensified. I always seemed to be on the wrong end of her sharp tongue. A week later, my uncle came home with a large plastic carrier bag. 'Come children,' he said. 'Here are your clothes for your first day back at school.'

He separated the white blouses and shirts, black trousers, skirts and blazers. 'Keep them folded now,' he said as he handed them out. 'You must be a credit to me.'

I waited for mine, but when the bag was empty I was still waiting.

'Why am I not getting any? It is my first day too,' I said.

My aunt scowled at me.

'In time, in time,' said my uncle.

The end of the week came, but still I had no uniform. On the Monday morning the others got dressed and ready for school. 'What am I to wear?' I asked my aunt.

She looked at me with distaste. 'School, why you want to go to school? Is education going to feed you? You eat too much. We have bills to pay. Why am I expected to keep a strange child for no money? How do you expect to stay in this house when you do not pay?'

For a moment I was too shocked to speak. 'But you took me here to educate me,' I said finally. 'And my parents gave you money.'

'You think they gave me enough? They do not know the cost of everything in this country. You came here illegally. How you expect to go to school? If the authorities find you here I will lose everything. You must work. Get a job.'

I could not believe what I was hearing. 'Work? My father never made me work. Not one hour.'

'You are not with your father now, Freshy. You will not go to the school my children go to.'

'Then am I going to a different school?'

She said nothing and turned away from me.

After the other children left, I decided to go to the park. As I reached the door, my aunt's voice cut across the room. 'Where do you think you're going?'

'Outside.' My hand stopped, my fingers barely touching the knob.

'No,' she shouted. 'You are trying to get me into trouble? People will see you. A child your age not at school. There will be questions asked. You have to stay indoors until the others come home.'

I went to turn on the TV. She snatched the remote from me and punched me. 'You are costing me more money! You know the cost of electricity? You will not watch TV in the day time.'

All that morning I stood at the window to pass some of the time, watching the cars drive by. In the days that followed, Aunt made me clean the toilet, scrub the stairs and do other distasteful jobs that no one else wanted to do. Sometimes I had to take care of the babies while my aunt and Basmah went out, or play with the little ones when they became fractious. I didn't mind that, I enjoyed their games and small arms around my neck.

My nightmares, however, became more frequent and more intense and often I would scream aloud. The family grew fed up with being wakened in the night and my uncle asked me about these terrors. When I told him in detail, he looked at his wife and she placed her hand on her mouth.

'It is the devil,' she whispered. 'The devil is in you stealing your soul. You must be a very wicked boy to have dreams like these. All the things that happened to you,

71

people see the devil in your eyes. No wonder they try to kill you.' She backed out of the room, her face a mask of horror.

After that I was not allowed to play with the babies. Basmah, too, believed I had the devil in me and kept the children away from me. I grew even more unhappy, believing all that had happened to me was my own fault and I could not understand what I had done that was so bad. Was it because, like my ammo, my skin was a paler shade than most other Bangladeshis? I wanted so much to talk to my family, but there was not enough credit in my phone and I was not allowed to use the Badour's landline.

One morning a stranger came to the house. He was European but did not sound English. Aunt went to the sideboard and brought out my passport which he studied. 'This will do,' he said, and handed her a wad of notes.

'What are you doing? That's my passport,' I shouted.

'You can get another one.' Aunt thanked the man and walked with him to the door, speaking in English.

Day after day, after my chores, I sat at the window watching the ever-changing weather. Sometimes the sky was blue with sunshine which never brought the searing heat it brought to Bangladesh, sometimes shifting clouds made shapes of animals or buildings, sometimes it rained and as the drops ran down the pane, I took bets in my head about which one would reach the bottom first.

As I yearned for my home and my family, I pressed my face against the cool glass and remembered how the heat moved aside for the monsoons, how the water drummed on the tin roof of our house and gushed from the gutters, how the rickshaw boys continued to work, their shoulders hunched, rain running from their hair, blinding their eyes. And when the wind rose and whined around the London flats, I closed my eyes and imagined palm trees bending away from the blast, their fronds whipping to and fro.

And once again, the past would begin to play itself out in the playground of my mind, like an old movie.

*It is the monsoons season and I want to go outside.*

*'You cannot go out,' my mother scolds. 'The rains will soon come and you will get wet.' But I ignore her and run for my friend Chandraj. Together we go to the cricket field. Above, purple and grey clouds roll across the sky and the air is quiet. Then it starts to rain, fast and furious. Water comes down in sheets, fills the day and the air and turns the dust on the ground into mud within seconds. We dance in the downpour, laughing. A'isha comes to the doorway of our house and shouts at me. 'You are getting covered in mud. I am not going to wash you.'*

*I don't care. Chandraj and I continue to dance and laugh until A'isha grabs my arm and drags me indoors. 'I am not going to wash you,' she repeats, but as I sit shivering before the fire, she returns with a basin of water and removes my clothes. She begins to sponge me all over. 'You must learn to do this yourself. When you get married your wife will not be as kind as I.'*

*My mother comes in with a plate of food and starts to feed me.*

The sharp voice of my aunt cut through my thoughts. 'Daydreaming again! All I do is work and Freshy stands at the window and daydreams. It is our turn to scrub the stairs. This is your job – but do not go outside.'

Every night I cried myself to sleep, until my pillow was soaking. I seldom found solace in in the dark hours as the horrors of my dreams lay waiting. I constantly nagged my aunt about going to school and each time I did, her temper grew worse. All day she complained about me. I was in her way. I was cheeky. I was eating too much. I had the devil in me and she did not want the devil in her house.

When the time approached for my parents' phone call, she grabbed my shirt at the shoulder, put her face close to mine and hissed, 'You had better tell them you are in education.'

I jerked from her. 'I am not going to lie. You promised to put me to school. Why are you not keeping that promise?'

Surely Abboo would put this right, I thought.

When the phone rang at the arranged time, I ran to answer it, but my aunt was there before me and Basmah stepped in front of me, barring my way.

'You will not speak to them,' she said in a low voice.

'He's not here,' I heard Aunt say, 'He is at activities the school puts on after classes. Yes, he's doing very well. Yes, I'll tell him.'

'Why did you not let me speak to them?' I cried.

'You will not do as I tell you. Unless you tell them you are in education, you will not speak to them ever again.'

I could not believe what I was hearing.

Later on that night, my parents rang again. This time Aunt told them I was in bed. 'Yes, he is tired. He has had a busy day at school.'

'Let me speak to my parents,' I shouted, but Aunt had already hung up.

'You go to prayers and then you lie. You are bad people,' I shouted.

'I have had enough.' She banged her fist on the table. 'You will have to live somewhere else. I should not have to put up with this.'

'You took me in. You got money from my abboo. You have to keep me.'

'Only way you can stay in this country is if you go to work.'

'Work? But I want to go to school.' As I said the words I knew they were true. In spite of my truancy in

Bangladesh, I genuinely wanted to do well in this country and make my parents proud.

She started shouting at Uncle. 'Get him out of here. Get him a job so he can pay his way. What good is he? He does not even like Rubana anymore. '

'Okay, okay,' said my uncle. 'Calm down. I will get him a job.'

'I will not work. If I'm not going to school, I want to go back to Bangladesh,' I said.

'If you go back, your parents will lose a lot of money,' said my uncle.

'They have already lost their money because you took it all.' My voice rose with my temper.

'What do you mean?'

'I know what they gave you. And I heard you talking. They are giving you more, aren't they? Where does that money go?'

Aunt came towards me, her face angry, her brows turned down, her arm pulled back as if to strike me. In her hand was a large serving spoon.

I squared my shoulders and met her gaze. 'So you want to kill me – okay you do that. Other people have tried and they couldn't.' My hands clenched into fists. I waited for the blow.

She stopped. Her eyes grew round. Her hand flew to her mouth. She gasped, stepped back, then ran past me to her bedroom.

'Do not worry,' my uncle said. 'What will happen will happen. It is your fate.' And the words of the old man came back to me. Aunt neither spoke to nor looked at me after that. All the time she walked around muttering and complaining to herself. I still played with the younger children after school, but Rubana and the adults mostly ignored me and always spoke in English. Every day when the others were at school I stared out of the window or cleaned the house. Once I tried to play with the babies.

'Keep him away from my children,' Basmah screamed to Auntie. 'The devil is in him.' She never spoke directly to me.

I was never allowed to speak to my parents. The whole family conspired against me, keeping me away from the telephone.

Aunt always made some excuse; I was out playing, I was at after-school activities, I was in bed. I wondered why my parents did not suspect that something was wrong, or worse still, did they believe that my life was so good that I no longer wanted to talk to them?

Eventually I gave in and agreed to tell my parents I was in education. It was the only way I was allowed to hear their voices.

The weather grew colder and one day I woke up to a sharp coldness and a strange silence in the air. The household was still asleep. It was dark, but not completely dark, it was never completely dark in London. The glow from the streetlamps polluted the sky. I rose and switched on the light. My breath hung before me like smoke. Curious, I crossed to the window and looked out into a strange white world with slow flakes drifting from the sky. It was the first time I had seen snow.

In spite of the cold I enjoyed playing with the kids I had come to know on the estate. Snowball fights, slides and sledging were novelties to me. Unfortunately the snow only lasted two days.

Then other things began to happen. Adorned trees with sparkling lights appeared in windows, programmes on television showed decorated shops and happy families with lots of food stacked on tables and a man dressed in red with a beard riding on a sleigh pulled by reindeers. One night a bunch of young people came round the door singing.

'What's going on?' I asked Uncle.

'This is how the Christians in the west celebrate the birth of Christ,' he said.

In Bangladesh we celebrate this day with a national holiday. Christians back home celebrate by planting banana trees.

Then came the new year. As the clock struck midnight, I could hear the shouting and cheering from street parties. I clutched the windowsill as I watched the rockets and fireworks in the distance. And I thought of new year back home in Bangladesh.

*The day before, our home will have been thoroughly cleaned. The new year will begin at dawn and my family and friends will be dressed in their best clothes. After prayers they will visit relatives, friends and neighbours and special foods will have been prepared and shared with guests. All over Bangladesh there will be singing, processions and fairs. Food stalls in the market place will be busier than usual. There will be folk-singing and traditional puppet plays. We have many foreign visitors during the Bengali new year.*

*I close my eyes and lose myself in the memories. I allow myself to be carried back, to feel the excitement as friends and neighbours come to the door with laughter and greetings. I can almost taste the sweetmeats Ammo has prepared. Later our family will go out and do our own visiting. Every door will be open and the scent of sweet spices will fill the air.*

*But wait, it is not yet time. Our new year is in April. I have been told this is the first day of January. And on this day Bangladesh also celebrates with a holiday from work.*

# Chapter 9

The months stretched and the air began to grow warmer and my days melted into each other. My life was filled with an intense loneliness. I'd been surrounded by love and kindness all my life, now I was shunned and treated as if I was evil. I began to live in my past, and the happy times I spent with my family. I saw myself swimming in the pond with my friends, getting into mud fights. I remembered A'isha scolding me, threatening not to wash me, but washing me anyway, while I laughed and pulled her hair.

One morning my uncle woke me early. 'Come on,' he said. 'After prayers we are going to an agency where they will find you work.'

I couldn't eat breakfast. My inside clenched. What kind of work were they going to make me do? When would I get a chance to tell the truth to my parents?

We climbed into his car. 'You told my dad lies. Why? Why did you do this thing?'

With the keys still in his hand he turned to face me. The pillows under his eyes never drooped so low. He sucked in his bottom lip and shook his head and his body sagged as if he was defeated. 'It's not me, it's my wife.'

'But you are the man. You must tell her what to do.'

He shook his head. 'Yes I am the man and I have to do what I can to provide for my family.'

'So you brought me here just to get my father's money?'

'I want a better life for my children.'

'But you have a house and a car and your children go to school. Why do you have to steal from us? You are a greedy person.'

He shrugged his shoulders and rubbed his hand over his face. 'We want the best for them. This was a way.'

'What about me?'

'You will survive.'

'Are you not scared for your soul? What's the point of praying when you do this?'

'Look at me. I am disabled, I cannot do much work. The money the state gives me is not enough.'

'Money from the state?' I was confused. Getting money from the state was not something that happened in Bangladesh.

'It's not enough. Look how many mouths I have to feed.'

'But your son goes to work.'

'In a restaurant; the pay is very poor.'

'But you can't steal my money. What about my family?'

'They will survive. I'm sorry, but what must be must be.'

'What if you were in my place? If I was your son?' I couldn't hold back the tears. My words tumbled over my tongue as my desperation grew.

He stared out of the window.

'I want to go home,' I said.

'That's impossible.' He shrugged and started the car. He didn't speak to me again as we drove. I don't remember much about that drive, only that I was trapped and had no control over what was happening to me. I remembered the lessons from the Qur'an. I remembered it said that all Muslims must respect each other. The Badours thought themselves to be good Muslims, yet they were treating me like this.

We stopped in front of a small shop which sold CDs and videos. Uncle led me through to the back where there was an office with a heavy-set man behind a desk. Looking up at us, the man blew out some smoke and then stubbed his cigarette in a heavy glass ashtray.

'What can I do for you?' he said.

Uncle introduced himself. 'We spoke on the telephone. It's all there.' And he handed the man an envelope.

'Is this your son?' The man stared at me for what seemed a long time, surprise written on his face. Finally he spoke again. 'He is too small. I cannot put a child that age out to work. What are you thinking?'

'He is my son. He is sixteen. He has been ill and it stunted his growth. '

I wanted to shout out the truth, but I felt trapped and afraid to speak.

The man was not satisfied. 'He does not look sixteen.'

'He is my son; surely I should know how old he is.'

'Why are you sending this child to work?'

My uncle leaned forward and rested his knuckles against the desk. 'You must help,' he said, lowering his voice. 'I am married for a second time and my new wife does not take to the son of my first marriage. It's bad for him in my house.'

The agency man shook his head. 'I don't like it.'

'I'll pay more money.' Uncle reached into his pocket and brought out a wad of money.  He counted out fifty notes and laid them on the desk.

The tone of the agency man's voice changed. 'This happens so often in our culture.' He shook his head. 'I know what it's like to have a wife with the tongue of a serpent. If you are sure this is best for him, I have a vacancy in a restaurant in Brighton. He will be able to wash dishes?'

'Of course he can. He washes dishes all the time at home.' My uncle stood up smiling, his body relaxing.

It was then I realised that everything in this country was about money.

That night my nightmares were worse than ever; flashes of different scenes filled my head. The shadows with long fingernails leaping at me, then the green field with swings, but children were throwing the swings at me trying to strike me, blonde-haired girls smiling at me and finally the old man, dressed in white like the High Imam, smiling, calming me, but he was gone in an instant, to be replaced by the shadows. I woke up exhausted. I must have woken the whole house with my screams, as in the morning no one would meet my eye and seemed to stay as far away as possible. Even the younger kids appeared afraid.

After prayers my uncle took me to one side. 'A man is coming to take us to where you are going to live. You will tell them that you are sixteen and that I am your father. When your parents phone, you will tell them you are in education. If you ever tell the truth, you will never see them alive again.' The regret from the day before had gone from his voice. His eyes and voice were hard. 'I *can* have them killed,' he said with enough strength that I believed him. And I knew then, that even if he didn't, his wife surely would.

The man came in a red car. My heart was lead, my tears rolled unheeded down my cheeks. Once again I was being taken into the unknown and I could not risk telling my parents.

As I left I turned to look at my cousins but they averted their eyes. Only Rubana met my gaze. She bit her lip. Her eyes were as hard as those of her mother. No one from that house said goodbye.

As the driver turned the key in the ignition, my uncle handed me a long narrow booklet. 'This is a pay-in book. You will earn £100 a week – cash. You must take it to the bank and give them the money and the book. Do you understand?'

I didn't, but nodded anyway.

'Good.' He settled in his seat. 'I'll show you where the bank is when we get to Brighton.'

We drove out from the city. This time I did not look with interest at the high buildings and busy streets. My eyes were clouded with tears, my heart tight with fear. Where was I going? What was going to happen to me?

# Chapter 10

In spite of my fear of the unknown, I was amazed to see the countryside of Britain. It was early summer and I estimate I must have been about nine months with the Badours. I could not get over how green everything was. And the houses, so different from Bangladesh, standing alone in their own gardens; sturdy healthy-looking animals in the fields; stretches of forests.

After several hours, we rounded a corner and in the distance I saw an expanse of blue water; more water in one place than I had ever seen, with the sun throwing sparkles from the surface, welcoming me to Brighton. It was the first time I had ever seen the sea. As we drove into town, I was amazed at what amounted to naked people. Girls with bikinis, men in trunks. They walked along the waterfront, eating ice-cream, towels slung over their arms. Apart from the fact that they were blatantly showing off their bodies, I could not understand why they were not cold. Even the heat of summer in England was cold to me. My heart lifted. We were away from the high buildings crowded together. My life might get better in this pretty place, I thought, because nothing could be worse than those last weeks with Uncle and Auntie. If only I had known.

We arrived at the restaurant at four o'clock in the afternoon. It was a big restaurant with many tables. A pleasant looking man approached us, smiling.

'Mr Bashir?' asked my uncle holding out his hand.

The man nodded and waited, questions in his eyes.

'You have been expecting us. I am Badour. This is my son,' said Uncle placing his hand on my shoulder. 'He is your new dish-washer.'

'This boy?' the restaurant owner said stepping back. 'What are you thinking? I cannot employ a child.'

My uncle repeated the words he said to the man at the employment agency.

'I don't know. He is so small, not fit for hard work.' Mr Bashir looked unsure.

'We were sent here. I cannot take him back now,' said Uncle. 'My wife won't have him in the house – what am I to do with him? He can wash dishes – anyone can wash dishes. He does it all the time at home.'

Mr Bashir put his hand to his chin, looked at me with sympathy, then appeared to make up his mind. 'I'll give him a trial,' he said.

'Good, good, that's all we ask.' My uncle relaxed and, without a word of goodbye, he turned and left.

'There is something not right about this. Tell me the truth now, because I do not like to be lied to. Is he your father?' asked Mr Bashir.

I nodded. Every fibre of my body screamed to tell the truth, but I was so afraid for my parents. I believed that the Badours would have them killed as they had threatened. I'm sure Mr Bashir was a good man who would have helped me, had I the courage to speak up then.

'And you are sixteen?'

I nodded again. He knelt down so that his eyes were level with mine. 'I will not forgive you if you lie.'

'I'm not lying,' I blurted out, although my heart was racing and I felt my pulse beat all the way up to my throat.

'We do need a dish-washer and we need him right now.' He took me upstairs and showed me the bathroom. 'You can wash your clothes in the basin on your time off.' Then he led me to a small room with three beds crowded into a cramped space and otherwise empty. Handing me a white shirt and black trousers, he told me to change and come back downstairs as soon as I was ready. Alone, I studied the room. There was a small window facing another building. The walls might have once been white, but now showed evidence of too much cigarette smoke. I did not want to stay here with strangers. I did not want to wash dishes. The trapped feeling crushed me and brought tears to my eyes. With very little English and nowhere to go, I could not run away. Slowly I unfolded the clothes which were much too big for me but pulled them on anyway, rolling up the trouser legs and the shirt sleeves.

When I went back downstairs, Mr Bashir sighed and shook his head. 'You cannot work like that. Go back and wear your own clothes. We have nothing to fit a child. Just stay in the kitchen, out of sight.'

After I returned, he took me to the kitchen. The smell was of spices, burning fat and smoke. In the sink the dishes were piled so high that I gasped. I had never seen so many dishes. Panic set in. Washing that mountain would take me forever.

Mr Bashir introduced me to the head chef, Jamal, a slim man with a white hat and an apron.

Jamal was in charge of the kitchen. 'What? A little boy? Why did you take a child on? How can he keep up with the work? I don't want a child.'

'Be kind to him,' said Mr Bashir. 'He's very young. Show him what to do. I want to help him and we have no one else.'

'Come then,' said the chef, but he did not look pleased. 'Have you ever worked in a restaurant before?'

Unable to speak, I shook my head.

'But you can wash dishes?'

I nodded.

He showed me how to cut the vegetables and when he was confident that I could do that, he led me to the stack of dishes. I could not reach the sink so he fetched a box for me to stand on. That first night, I washed dishes until three o'clock in the morning. All the time people shouted at each other and at me.

'Have you got those plates clean yet?'

'This fork still has food on it.'

'More plates, more plates,'

'Hurry up!'

As their tempers rose, I dropped plates in my haste and each dropped plate earned me a slap from one of the kitchen hands. 'You won't be here very long if you cannot work faster,' they shouted. I hated every minute but I was afraid and trapped and I didn't know what to do.

By knocking-off time, my hands were sore and wrinkled, my feet and legs ached with standing so long, and my back felt as if it would break. I was so tired that night, yet, even after the others had fallen into noisy slumber, I couldn't sleep. I thought of Jasmine, our servant girl, hands deep in water, washing our dishes. I thought of the heat, the dust, the laughter; a time when I had never considered for a moment that I would one day be forced to do women's work. In our culture, men are not allowed to do what is considered women's work.

I buried my face in the pillow so that my sobs would not fill the room and wake the others. I thought of Abboo, how kind he was, how gentle. Only once he had raised his voice in anger at me. I had fallen out with my friend and had called him a dirty Hindu. Abboo grabbed me by the front of my shirt. 'Don't you ever make racist comments. You are no better than anyone else. Go and apologise to Chandraj.'

I cried then, more hurt by my father's disappointment in me than if he had beaten me. A'isha came and wiped my tears. Recalling her soft hands and words brought on a fresh storm of weeping. By daylight I could have wrung out my pillow and I still had not slept.

At eight o'clock in the morning I was dragged from bed. 'We start at nine,' said Mahmud, one of the kitchen hands who shared my room. 'I hope you do better today.'

Then began the daily grind. I had to work until one o'clock, then I had two hours rest, which I spent in bed. I was told I would get one day off a week.

The second night, I cried myself to sleep. And then the nightmares began. I was pulled roughly awake by Mahmud.

'Why are you making this noise?' he shouted. 'We work hard and need our sleep. Be quiet.' I was afraid to sleep for the rest of the night. The next day I was so tired I wondered how I would ever mange to work. By the third night I was so exhausted that I collapsed onto my bed and knew nothing till morning.

On my time off, I hand-washed my few pieces of clothing in the basin in the lavatory or lay on the bed watching the sky through the small square of window. I was too scared of the unknown to go outside alone, except to pay my money into my uncle's account as I had been instructed.

Finally my parents phoned me on my mobile and I could not hold back the tears. Believing the threats of my uncle, I could not tell them the truth, yet it swelled in my chest. 'I'm so happy to hear from you,' I said, giving reason for my sobs.

Abboo asked me, 'What did you learn today?'

I did not want to lie. I could not tell the truth. 'I learned how to cook,' I said. It was not a lie. Not exactly.

# Chapter 11

I had been working there for six weeks when everything changed. The tandoori chef left and a new chef came into our lives. His name was Aabzari Hossain. From the minute I laid eyes on him, I could not understand the instant dislike I felt for him. He was presentable enough, tall, over six feet, slightly chubby with narrow black eyes and he too came from Bangladesh. He introduced himself as Hoss and everyone else seemed to like him. He put himself out of his way to be friendly and helpful. The first time his eyes found me, he smiled – not at me, more to himself. All the time I felt him looking at me and smiling and I did not feel comfortable with that smile.

The first night he shared my room, I cried out for Abboo and Ammo as my nightmare took hold and he slammed a pillow over my face. I woke up struggling and desperate for air. Then I heard Mahmud's voice, 'What are you doing – you'll kill him.' He must have pulled Hoss off, because the next minute the pillow had gone and I was desperately sucking in air. Mahmud fetched me a glass of water. 'There was no need for that,' he said, shooting a warning glance at Hoss. Trembling and terrified, I did not shut my eyes again that night.

The next afternoon, during my time off, as I lay on my bed trying to lose myself in sleep, Hoss came into the room. The bed dipped as he lowered himself beside me. I started away from him, pressing myself against the wall and covering my head with my hands.

'Relax. I'm not going to hurt you,' he said.

I peered at him from between my fingers.

'There is something wrong here.' He gently eased my hand away from my face. 'I do not believe you are sixteen.'

I bit my lip to stifle my sounds of sorrow.

'Tell me the truth.' He placed his hand on my shoulder. His touch was the first gentle contact from another human in so long and it released a fresh bout of weeping. I wanted to speak, to pour out my fears and give them to an adult I could trust, but I could not trust Hoss. I lay rigid, staring at him, waiting for what might come next.

'I was angry last night; half asleep. I realise you must be very upset.' He said this gently. 'I'm so sorry. I want to make it up to you. Let me help you.'

I didn't want him to reach me, yet he sounded so sincere and I was so desperate for a spot of kindness that my feelings became jumbled. But I could not tell him anything. I could not put my parents in danger.

'Look,' he repeated, his voice still low. 'Trust me. I want to help you.'

And the secret swelled and filled me up until I could contain it no longer.

'That man who brought you here is not your dad, is he?'

I looked at him and saw him through a blur of tears. Could he really help me? Unable to hold back the words, the truth gushed from me as if a dam had been broken. 'No. He is a bad man. He brought me here to educate me and then stole my parents' money.'

Hoss eased himself into a more comfortable position his eyes gleaming. 'I think you have a lot more to tell me. Start with the dreams.'

I described the dreams and that my aunt told me it was the devil. He smiled then, a self-satisfied smile. It had felt so good to finally let go of the lie, that I relaxed and told him the whole dismal story.

'Come.' He took my hand and pulled me upright. 'We are going to phone your parents and tell them what has been happening. You are not to worry. I have friends in your village. They will look out for your family.'

I was happy but scared. Finally I experienced a ray of hope. I was a child, desperate, unhappy, trapped and friendless and here was an adult offering to help me.

I stood by Hoss's side as he phoned my parents and related my story. Everything would be alright now, I told myself as he spoke. Then he gave me the phone. At the sound of my Abboo's voice, my body melted and the emotion gushed forth. Abboo, too, was crying. 'You must go to the police,' he said. 'Get out of there. You must come home.'

'Yes, yes, I want to come home.' There was so much relief at finally being able to tell my parents the truth I could hardly stammer the words.

Hoss indicated that he wanted to talk some more and I handed the phone over. 'He cannot go home. The Badours have sold his passport. He must never go to the police; he is in this country illegally and they will throw him in prison and he will never get out again. A British prison is a terrible place – he will be in great danger. Do not worry about him. I have a cousin who is a school teacher and he has children the same age. I will take him to live there and he will get good schooling.'

His smooth voice ran on as my hope of returning to Bangladesh died. Then he asked my father how much money he had, what he owned, how much more he could afford to pay. He listened for a while and then said, 'In that case Abdul will have to work for longer. He must make money for education, and he will send you half of his wages. That should help you out of your predicament.'

After he hung up, he turned to me. 'Your father has no money left; he gave it all to the Badours. Every penny. You will have to work at least six months to pay for your schooling. Also we must send money to your parents. Life is hard for them now.'

'They took my wages too.' My heart filled with anger towards my so called 'uncle' and 'aunt'. Not only had they stolen from my parents, but they had also stolen from me.

Hoss nodded. 'We will sort this. Have you got the number for their phone?'

I didn't, but I knew their names and where they lived. It didn't take Hoss long to find the number.

He phoned my uncle and aunt and shouted at them in English.

'They have been stealing your money,' he told me. 'Next week, give it to me. I will send half to your parents and save half for you. But you must not tell anyone. If you do, you will be sent back to live with your aunt and uncle and they will beat you. They won't keep you for nothing – they might kill you.'

Hoss showed me nothing but kindness and he had promised to help me; why then did my insides tighten whenever he came near? But I was guided by him as I had no one else. I knew the Badours did not want me back, and was afraid of what would happen if I was sent there.

For a couple of weeks all was well. Hoss arranged his day off to coincide with mine which meant we were constantly together. He took me out and all round Brighton, but I was too depressed at that time to enjoy anything. I was so tired after my restless nights that I only wanted to lie in bed. All the time he questioned me until he found out everything about my life. 'If you are ever caught by the police,' he told me, 'show them your scars. Tell them how your life is in danger. Tell them that your parents are dead – that way it will be better for you.'

My wages were now paid into Hoss's account and there was nothing I could do other than trust him.

When my parents phoned, they said they'd received the money, but they were still very worried about me. I was pleased that Hoss had kept his promise. Now that I had some hope for the future, I was happier. I became so grateful to Hoss, I began to look on him as my saviour. I told my parents not to be sad, Hoss was a good man who had rescued me and everything would be alright.

I have since found out that Hoss only sent them money for the first six weeks; I believe that was only to earn their trust. From then on, he kept it all. Now I realise he had been grooming me for what was to come.

# Chapter 12

Six weeks later, on Friday, we walked along the street towards the bank so that I could pay my money into Hoss's account.

'Come along, let's take a little detour,' he said. 'Have you ever been inside a casino?'

'What's a casino?' I asked.

'Come I'll show you.' He pointed to a building we had passed before. There was music coming from the door and people wandering in and out.

'Will we go to the bank first?' I said, eager to have the money safely on its way to my parents.

'We'll go later, come away.'

Inside the building were machines and tables and coloured wheels that spun around.

I was not allowed into the main room, but had to sit in the foyer. After half an hour Hoss returned. 'Give me your money.' He held out his hand.

'But why?' I said.

'Just give it to me.' His voice was hard and impatient. This was no longer the kind spoken Hoss who had been slowly winning my trust. I shrank against the wall and took the notes from my wallet. 'All of it,' he snapped.

'That is all of it,' I said.

'There's more in there.'

'It's from home.' My fingers closed around the five taka note I had found the day I had met the old man.

He snatched it from me, studied it and shoved it back at me. 'You can keep this,' he said, with a snort.

I folded it and tucked it into the furthest pocket of the wallet. It would have hurt me more to lose that note than all the English money he had stolen from me. It was my link with home, my link with that one special meeting.

An hour later he came out again, his brows screwed down and his lips pressed in a tight line. Pinning me with a stare, he held out his hand. 'Give me your phone.'

When I took it from my pocket, he snatched at it. 'Now,' he said, 'we will go and see your uncle in London and get your money back. When we go there, don't say a word. Leave everything to me.' He spun away and headed for the bus-stop with me running to keep up with him.

I didn't know then what he'd done with my money, but it was the last time my parents or I saw any of it. From that moment on, the kind face of Hoss disappeared and I only felt his anger. Yet, that day, I still trusted him to get my money back from my uncle and aunt. I did want to see Rubana and the other kids again, but when we arrived, they were still at school.

When my uncle answered the knock, his face registered first shock and then fear. 'What do you want?' he shouted and made to slam the door.

Hoss stepped forward pushing his shoulder against the door and elbowed his way past.

My aunt rushed from the kitchen. 'What is he doing here?' Her eyes travelled from me to Hoss then back again. 'What do you want?' Her hands frantically twisted the dishcloth they held.

'We want the money you stole from the boy,' said Hoss.

'We stole no money,' my uncle said.

Hoss laughed. 'I know exactly what you have been doing and now his parents do as well.'

'Come into the kitchen,' said Uncle. 'I have to explain.'

I tried to follow, but they shut the door in my face. I sat, straining my ears, but all I could hear was the raised voices, often in English and too fast for me to identify individual words. The shouting went on for some time.

Then the voices calmed and turned to laughter. When they left the kitchen all three had smiles on their faces.

For the second time, when I left that house, no one said goodbye. I never saw my aunt and uncle again.

'Did you get my money?' I asked Hoss as we walked towards the bus stop.

'You don't have to bother about that. You belong to me now.' His voice was sharp and invited no further questions.

I knew at that moment that I was once again in a trap. I never found out what was said in that kitchen or what happened to my money.

The cold seeped through the streets and into our bedroom above the restaurant. The hope that had flourished in my heart had withered and died and, right then, I wanted to die too.

Then came the run-up to Christmas. I had no knowledge of this type of Christmas except what I had seen on television and in the surrounding streets last year when I lived in the Badour's home. The staff decorated the tree, hung decorations, and placed crackers and streamers on the tables. People came in to eat, happy and laughing, couples and families with children. They pulled the crackers, wore paper hats and drank wine, their joy making my own wretchedness more acute.

The New Year was no different. I could see the fireworks in the distance, hear the cheers after the bells and wished I could be among the revellers. The next day was the only day the restaurant closed and everyone had a holiday.

Back in Bangladesh, there would also be a holiday for this day.

I missed my home and the love of my parents so much it was like a physical pain in my chest. Hoss gave me my phone at specific times and, standing over me, he told me what to say. My family believed I was saving for my school fees and was happy and that any tears were because of homesickness. The truth was so different. I no longer felt emotion. I stopped eating and began to lose my hair. My hands were raw and red from all the dish-washing. As I grew thinner, my hands began to weep and the rents went septic.

By now I was completely under Hoss's control. I was not at any time out of his sight. He confused me by being pleasant and angry in turns. By January, the other restaurant workers began to comment on my health. They were often kind to me and, looking back, I realise how helpless they were even if they had reservations about my relationship with Hoss. They had families to feed and I was just another boy from Bangladesh, a country where child labour is still commonplace.

I believe it was only because of their comments that Hoss pretended concern. One Friday, after we received our pay, he took me to a chemist and asked the lady there if she had any cream for my skin. She looked at me, then my hands. I understood very little English at this stage but I recognised the word *doctor* and the shock in her voice. Pretty and clean-looking, she had blond hair and blue eyes and she smelt of flowers. She spoke to me softly and I wished I could talk to her, stay with her and leave Hoss behind. I thought she was beautiful and I could not look away from her face.

Hoss spoke to her in English and she nodded as if his answer satisfied her. She led us to another room where she set me on a chair, knelt in front of me and rubbed cream on my hands. Her touch was soft, her voice gentle. Although I did not understand much of what she said, I wanted to go on listening to her words forever.

Turning her attention to Hoss, she stood up and handed the tube of cream to him and a great empty wave washed over me. Again I recognised the word '*doctor*' and '*soon*'.

'I will,' promised Hoss.

When she said goodbye, she stroked my head and smiled at me.

'Do you like her?' asked Hoss as we walked away.

'Yes. What did you tell her?' I asked.

'That you were my son, that we had just arrived in the country and I had not had time to register with a doctor.'

'Will you take me to a doctor?'

'I will look after you for the rest of your life. You are not to be ungrateful.' He held out his hand. 'Give me your wages.'

I pulled the packet from my pocket.

'Can I have something for myself?' I asked. 'I need a jacket. I'm cold.'

He slapped me, hard enough to make my ears ring.

'Come on – I will show you better ways to spend your money.'

# Chapter 13

He took me to a narrow, dark alley where tall, black buildings crowded out what little light the misshapen moon offered. The wind moaned and hurled litter along the street.

'Stay here,' he said, pulling a torn piece of newspaper from around his ankles. He stepped in a puddle splintering the sulphur light that reflected from the lamp-posts and he swore. Opposite to where I stood was an open door through which various men were coming and going. Hoss entered that door and nodded a greeting to others, their faces highlighted in the smoky light. White men, black men, West Asian men, East Asian men, well-dressed men, scruffy men. They looked at me as they passed and averted their eyes. I pressed myself against the stone; the bitter surface turning my body to ice, freezing out the will to live. Other men hanging around the alley stared at me. Then a guy, as black as night, tall and broad with eyes which appeared red, came out and approached me. I had never seen such a man and fear gripped me, stopping my breath. He grinned at me, his wide mouth all teeth, then he nodded slowly and left.

A few minutes later Hoss returned with the ugliest woman I had ever seen. Her hair was blonde and wispy, barely covering her head. Her eyes were too close together, as if they were fighting for space over her bulbous nose. She pursed thick lips and her chin disappeared in several layers of fat. Her shoulders seemed to swallow her neck. Large breasts threatened to spill from a low, tight, sequined top and the heavy upper half of her body tapered to narrow hips and legs that reminded me of the chickens back home.

She looked at me and shouted something to Hoss, all the time shaking her head. I recognised the words, 'No, no no,' and, 'too young.'

Hoss's shoulders quickly raised and lowered in a shrug. 'As you wish,' he said, lifting his palms upward and they both returned inside. Time stretched and lingered and I wrapped my arms around myself in a vain attempt to gain warmth. After a time, the woman reappeared and offered me a biscuit. When I reached to take it, she noticed my hands. She covered her mouth with pudgy fingers and screamed. She babbled on at some length, words spilling out, too fast for me to understand. Unable to stop myself, my legs, frozen to the point of numbness, buckled and I started to cry.

'Oh poor boy,' the woman said, and flung her arms around me, her great breasts in my face so that I could hardly breathe. She did not smell fresh and sweet like the lady in the chemist; her smell was heavy and thick and made me gag.

'Come here.' With an arm around me she guided me inside and through another door where people were watching a film. The room was warm and sickly-sweet. On the screen naked bodies writhed and moaned and the audience grunted and fidgeted, not noticing me at all. The woman pushed me forward and into a corridor where she indicated that I must wait. In spite of the welcome warmth, I sat shaking and crying. Distressed children must have been a common sight, as none of the adults who passed gave me a second glance.

Time stretched and the space grew airless so that I could hardly breathe. Eventually Hoss reappeared wriggling into his jacket and he seemed in good spirits. 'Come, we have to go. We have a bus to catch.' I followed him into a street glistening with the cast of streetlights and where the sharp air hit me; its icy blast penetrating my T-shirt.

Hoss squeezed my shoulder so that it hurt. 'Do you want to die?' he asked, his eyes like black stone piercing my soul.

I shook my head.

'If you tell anyone about this – that is exactly what will happen to you.'

Once more the truth was frozen in my heart.

# Chapter 14

One night, when the others were asleep and I lay weeping, my face pressed into the pillow so no one would hear, Hoss came over and lay beside me. His breath was hot and fast on my neck and he started to fondle me and I knew what he wanted to do. I scrambled away from him and he pulled me back against him. Here there was no Bahir to come and rescue me, no one at the end of a phone. My muffled screams and struggling woke the others and someone reached for the light. Hoss caught my eyes in the sulphur glow from the street light outside and drew the side of his hand across his throat before the yellow glare flooded the room.

'What's going on?' Mahmud, one of my room-mates, sat up, his hair on end, his eyes bleary.

'He had another nightmare,' Hoss said. 'I have been trying to comfort him.'

'Is this true?' asked Mahmud.

I nodded. I was crying too hard to speak and too afraid to deny it.

Mahmud angled his head slightly, as if he were suspicious. I hesitated, glanced at Hoss, saw the warning in his eyes. I couldn't tell whether Mahmud believed him or not, but with my denial, there was little he could do.

'Yes, I had a nightmare,' I lied.

After that I lived in a constant state of fear. Hoss's very eyes on me made my hand shake and my voice sticky. His presence in the same room tightened a throat already raw with tears. My body no longer craved food. Every mouthful made me sick. I grew so weak that my legs shook like saplings in the wind and my skin stretched across my bones, but worst of all, any hope of escape from this drudgery had died. I was often ill. By this stage I didn't care whether I lived or not and dragged myself through each day, growing ever weaker.

By now the other staff were constantly commenting on the state of my health, but with mouths to feed and jobs to keep, they were powerless to help. Hoss, the eternal nice guy, constantly spoke about his concern for me and that I should not be working in these conditions at my age. When he said he wanted to take me away for a break, no one was surprised.

'Later,' he said to me, 'we'll ask the manager for some time off.' I looked around the kitchen desperately, willing someone to intervene, but they were all intent on their work, and paid no attention.

After the evening shift was over he took me through to the restaurant to see the manager.

'I worry about Abdul,' he said. 'Look at him. He is not well.' His voice was smooth and persuasive.

The manager had not seen me for a few weeks and his eyes widened in shock. He knelt down so that he was level with me. 'Do you feel ill, Abdul?' There was genuine concern in his voice. I'm sure that if I had been able to tell him the truth he would have helped me and I would have spared myself years of pain, but by this time I was totally under Hoss's control and terrified by his threats. Without any will of my own, I only shook my head.

The manager looked at Hoss and lifted his hands in a despairing gesture. 'He is very young, but what can I do? We are so busy here and his father wants to put him to work.'

'Why don't I take him away for the weekend? I'm sure he will improve with a good rest.' Hoss set a hand on my shoulder. It was light and fatherly and made me squirm.

The manager smiled. 'You are a good man,' he said to Hoss. 'This is what the boy needs. Take good care of him.'

I wanted to beg him not to let me go, tried to plead with my eyes, but my terror of Hoss held me in its grip.

'You go,' said the manager, 'I will not take anything from your wages.'

About ten o'clock that night, Hoss took me to a hotel by the sea front. It was fairly run down, not like the others in the town. There were two beds in the room and, too weak to do anything else, I lay down on one, rolled into a ball and pressed myself against the wall, prepared to scream if he touched me. Hoss ignored me for which I was thankful. About ten minutes after we arrived, there was a knock on the door.

'Hello, come on in.' Hoss's voice was loud and friendly. I opened my eyes. Two men, one white, one black and a young girl came in. The girl was slight and fair-haired and looked no older than my sister. I noted the same fear in her eyes that I held in my heart. Nevertheless, she laughed at the things they said, but her laughter sounded forced and unnatural and was belied by the tear-drops quivering on the end of her lashes. I wanted to grab her hand and run out of there. My own helplessness overwhelmed me. I didn't know what to do. If the newcomers noticed I was there, which they must have done, they did not mention it.

When the men started to fondle the girl, I felt sick. Unable to stand what I was witnessing, I ran into the toilet and shut the door. Then the noises started. The laughter, the creaking bed, the curses. From time to time she screamed and begged for them to stop but her pleas were met by more laughter. I wrapped the towel round my head in a desperate effort to block out the sounds.

Then there was silence for a beat. One of the guys banged on the door and when I let him in he used the toilet and went out again. Then the noises started again. In desperation, I climbed into the bath where I curled up as tightly as I could and held my ears. The main fear I had was that they would come for me next.

Time passed. Then the girl came in, her face red and puffy, her cheeks streaked with tears. She looked at me and touched my face and said something in English.

I had learned a few more words by that time, enough to ask her if she was alright. She shook her head and said, 'No, but I have no choice.'

By then it was morning.

My 'break' sent me further into depression and despair of what my life had become.

I hated Hoss with a vengeance and was terrified of him. He relieved me of every penny I earned and had me completely under his control, yet he showed a very different face to the public. Everyone respected Hoss and thought he was the nicest guy.

Desperation drove me to tell someone what he was really like. Nothing he could do to me could be worse than this hell he was making me live and from the concerned way the staff often looked at me, I mistakenly supposed that someone would believe me. I tried to tell the head chef, who had been kind to me in the past, but he turned on me, furious. He slapped me and I knew I had made a mistake. 'Why are you telling lies?' he shouted. 'Hoss has been so kind to you. You are an evil boy.'

That night, Hoss took me upstairs, put his hands around my throat, slammed me so hard against the wall that my teeth rattled. 'Listen you shit-head, I will not stand for you making trouble. If you ever...ever... try anything like that again I will have your parents killed first and then I will kill you – slowly.

It was no use. No one would help me. I felt as though I was no longer alive, that I was just a shell, moving automatically from one day to the next. I'd even stopped crying; my tears had all been spent.

Sleep constantly evaded me. Early one morning, before the others awoke, I grabbed my stuff and crept from the restaurant. Where I was going or what I was going to do, I had no idea. I ran and ran for what seemed like hours until I found myself on top of a cliff. Down below were jagged rocks and beyond that, a golden beach. The sea rolled slowly over the sand, white ruffles at its edges. Above me the sun warmed the air and the breeze gentled through my hair and rustled the grass at my feet. People were walking on the beach with their children, playing, kicking a ball, wading in the quiet water. Their happiness only made me feel more desolate and empty. A man swung a little boy onto his shoulders and memories of my own Abboo tore me in two. I was so far away from home and from my family and the misery in my heart had never been worse. I was free, but where could I go? My English was poor, I had no passport and if I went to the police I would be put in prison, where I would be beaten daily and raped by guards until I died, or so Hoss had told me. Furthermore, my parents would be killed. Unable to cope with this existence, my only escape was to take my own life. I shuffled closer and closer to the cliff edge, steeling myself for the jump. As I stared at the rocks below, I heard my Abboo's voice in my head. *'Our prophet has taught us that it is a sin to kill. Life is sacred. Every life – even your own.'*

Below me I saw a baby bird, too young to fly. It had slipped off the ledge and was hanging onto a branch by its beak. The mother was screeching and flying around frantically. As I watched, the chick tried and tried to get back onto the ledge and I took it as a sign. If the bird falls to its death, I thought, I too will fall and be free. Eventually, with one desperate flapping of wings, the bird managed to pull itself back on the ledge. This little bird had fought so hard for survival and here was I planning to end it all. And I remembered the words of the old man.

*'What will happen will happen. It is your fate.'* I threw myself down on the grass and sobbed until I was drained and my body was sore.

It was the memory of the old man's words and the promise that I would return to Bangladesh one day that made me force my unwilling legs to move and carry me back to the restaurant. I had nowhere else to go. This was my fate and I would try somehow to survive. That day I was three hours late for work. I had a lump on my head and a bruise on my face where Hoss had banged me against the wall the night before.

Expecting Mr Bashir to be angry, I said I was sorry for being late, that I had gone for a walk on the cliffs and had slipped and fallen but that I was alright now. He wasn't angry; he was concerned.

He opened the till and gave me £120. My wages plus an extra £20. 'You have to tell me the truth,' he said.

'I am telling the truth,' I told him.

He did not look convinced. 'I think I'm doing my best for you by employing you. I think you are better here than at home. But you should be in school. I want to help you.'

He waited.

The truth swirled in my head and my heart but the words froze in my throat.

Again he asked me if I was alright and what had happened.

Why didn't I tell him then? Why did I lie to the very man who was trying to help me?

My fear was that he mightn't believe me. Bashir appeared to like Hoss and they often laughed together – Hoss had that way with him; a way of getting people to trust him. And after all these months he had worn me down, destroyed my sense of self-worth, and furthermore, memories of the chef's reaction and my subsequent punishment stilled my tongue.

# Chapter 15

It's hard for me to estimate how many days or weeks or even months passed. Time had little relevance in my world. Days rolled into struggling days, nights into sleepless nights. I did my work and slept when I could.

Then one day Hoss came to me and said, 'It's time you went to school. Phone your parents, tell them you need your birth certificate.'

With every word he spoke, I knew he was lying, but I had no choice but to do as he said. He handed me my phone and instructed me on what to say. I had to tell my parents that I'd now saved enough money to go to school and once I was there they would not be able to contact me for six months. Every fibre of my body screamed to tell them the truth but Hoss stood so near I could feel his breath on my cheek. Words were difficult as my throat was full of tears. Abboo asked me if I was alright but I replied that I was happy but missed them so much. Once the phone-call was over, Hoss put my mobile in his pocket and told me all the lies were for my own good.

Life carried on as before until my birth certificate arrived. As soon as he had me alone, Hoss snatched it from me. 'You won't need this,' he said. 'You belong to me now.' I found out later that he changed my date of birth to make me older.

Every day Hoss phoned my parents and gave them a false report of how I was progressing. They trusted him to do the best for me.

I said nothing. I had become an empty shell that functioned like a robot. What will happen will happen; the words spun in my head. The dreams still came nightly but now they were getting worse. I was walking along the road between the paddy fields and the shadows were grabbing me, then the dream would change and I was in a room being beaten and blood splattered the walls and flowed over the floor. A flash of blonde haired girls smiling at me, then shadows covering me again, blood dripping from their mouths and, suddenly, the old man, smiling and serene, in a sitting position, sitting on nothing. In a flash he would be gone and I was back in the horror. And so, sweating and twisting, I somehow fought my way through the nights. And every night, I held the locket, and gained comfort from the memory of my Ammo's parting words, '*Keep this always, my son. It will guide you safely back to us one day.*

One day, after the morning shift, Hoss took me to Mr Bashir and said, 'Abdul had a letter today, his parents want him back. They've asked me to take him home.'

'No. I cannot let him go unless his father comes for him.' Bashir watched me as if waiting for a response.

Hoss shook his head. 'I have found out many distressing things,' he said. 'That man is not Abdul's father.' He told him what my 'uncle' had done and my real age. 'I am going to help him. You see how thin he is, how bad his hands. This boy is ill. I am going to take him to a doctor and give him to my cousin who is a teacher and he will educate him. I have been in touch with his parents in Bangladesh and they are happy about this.'

Mr Bashir crouched before me and stared into my eyes. 'Is this true?'

I nodded and wanted to cry, but the tears had found a way of building up behind my eyes without spilling.

'Why did you lie to me? I could have helped you,' he said. 'I'm so disappointed in you. Have I not been good to you? Why is it that you could not come to me?'

'I'm sorry. I was afraid.'

'You don't have to go with Hoss. I will see you get to a doctor.'

'Can't you see he is ill.' Hoss' voice became edgy. 'See how he shakes. Look at his hands. He cannot work anymore.'

'What do you say, Abdul?' asked Mr Bashir. 'You are welcome to stay with me.'

'I want to go with Hoss.' The words were like bile on my tongue, but by then he had me so much in his grip and afraid for my parents that I would say anything.

I realise now that perhaps Bashir did not trust Hoss as much as I thought, as he still hesitated. Hoss offered him the phone. 'His real parents want me to look after him – here ask them yourself.'

Bashir shook his head and sighed. He went to the till and took out an extra £100. 'This is for you.' He handed it to me. 'Buy yourself a jacket. It's cold out there.' His eyes still looked worried. I believe he was a good man who would have saved me then, but what could he do when I continued to say the words Hoss put in my mouth?

Before we reached the train station, Hoss demanded the £100 from me. I didn't argue. As I removed the money from my wallet, he noticed the five taka note once again. 'All of it. You won't be needing money where you're going.'

With more reluctance than I had parted with any money before, I passed him the note.

'Pah,' he said. 'Have you still got that? What good is Taka in this country? It's worth nothing. Keep it.' He handed it back to me. Memories of the old man and the day I found the five taka swirled in my head. Who was that man? Why did he keep appearing to me? Was he watching over me even now? I slipped the note back into my wallet.

By the time we arrived in London, it was one o'clock in the morning. Hoss took me to a dark street. 'We go in the back way,' he said, and led me up an ally.

The wind sighed past red brick buildings with boarded up windows on one side and large steel doors with heavy locks on the other. Old newspapers and other debris rolled and lifted and gathered behind large refuse containers. He knocked on a scarred door, four sharp raps which matched the beat of my heart.

I counted each breath as the footsteps within the house drew nearer and the door groaned opened a fraction. An apparition peered out and then the door opened all the way. My body went cold. It was as if an evil presence passed from that house and draped around me.

The man who stood before us was bent and skinny with long stringy hair the colour of rotting rope. In the sulphur light that hit the planes of his face, I could see his teeth when he spoke; long and black, like mouldering tombstones, some missing, lumps of brown gunge settling round his gums. My first impression was that he'd been eating shit. He smelt strongly of smoke and alcohol and something else – something sickly-sweet and cloying. He greeted Hoss as if he knew him well and beckoned us to follow him.

Although I could not speak English, I understood a lot of what was said and Shit-Teeth's accent was not British. He guided us through a dark corridor and up three flights of stairs. I wanted to run, but even if there had been the opportunity, my legs would never have carried me. The light came from a single bulb hanging several floors above us, the wire draped with cobwebs.

Shit-Teeth stopped at a door, scarred and broken as if someone had put a foot through it at one time. 'In here,' he said. He pushed me into the room and slammed the door. The key turning in the lock echoed through the ensuing silence. Through a small window in the far wall, faint light from the street outside filtered in. Graffiti provided the only decoration on the walls and the smell was thick and heavy.

My legs, weak and shaking, folded beneath me and I sank onto a sticky, damp carpet.

I looked around. Through the gloom, I saw a mattress against the far wall with a pillow and blanket. A bucket sat beside a large square sink with a single tap. Apart from that, there was no furniture. The smell in here was of hopelessness and decay.

Weak and afraid, I crawled to the mattress and lay there. Close to, the stench of stale urine, vomit and sweat was identifiable, but I was too exhausted to care.

From outside the room there were noises, voices and footsteps; many people coming and going.

Eventually the door opened and Shit-Teeth, little more than a crooked silhouette, beckoned to me. 'Come get shower; you stink.'

He led me to a bathroom with a stained bath and a bowl with excrement smeared across its rim. 'Get cleaned up,' he ordered. 'Then you have food.' He handed me a small, torn towel.

'Where's my bag?' I asked. 'I need clean clothes.'

'Forget clothes. And no shoes. Give me shoes.'

I removed my trainers and he snatched them from me.

From the pocket of my track-suit bottoms, the edge of the wallet was visible. 'What have we here?' he said and, leaning forward, he pulled it out and began to go through the contents.

'Give me my wallet.' The loss of the taka note stabbed my soul more than anything else.

'You get later.' He pushed it into his pocket.

After I had washed in cold water and without soap, I did my best to dry myself with the rag of a towel and peered around the door.

'You finished?' Shit-Teeth had been waiting for me.

'My clothes,' I shouted.

'You have,' he said, sounding irritated. 'And keep towel.'

I was grateful that he hadn't seen the locket, still around my neck. If so he had no doubt he would have stolen that also.

I was so cold, I had no option than to dress in the curry-smelling shirt and trousers I had thrown in a corner. Then I stepped into the hallway. By this time I was so weak I had to hold on the wall to remain upright.

Shit-Teeth grabbed my arm and took me along the dark corridor and to the kitchen where he gave me a plate of cereal without milk. Dirty dishes littered the sink. Black fingerprints decorated the front of the fridge. Burnt pans sat atop the cooker and fat ran down the oven door. Some substance on the floor stuck to my bare feet. Even the bowl from which I ate had been used before, but I was too hungry to care. Then he took me back to the room.

'Why you put me here?' I said.

'This your room. Here you stay.'

What was the point in giving me a shower, I thought. The room smelled worse than I did. I tried to put my views into words with my limited English. He pushed me roughly through the doorway.

'I need my wallet – please,' I cried.

'You get later.'

'Where's Hoss?'

'He will come when he needs you.'

'When?' I shouted, but the door slammed in my face, the key grated in the lock and Shit-Teeth had gone.

For the first time in so long, I felt the desperate need to pray for the strength to somehow help me to make it through one more night. I folded the towel to use as a prayer mat and tumbled forward onto my face. I was too weak to kneel.

I must have fainted as the next thing I remember was lying on the towel, cheek against the carpet. I was cold and stiff. Somewhere from outside the sounds of a clock striking the hour assaulted my ears. Meagre daylight from the window slanted across my face. It was morning.

# Chapter 16

As I lay there, too stiff and miserable to move, Shit-Teeth came in and asked if I was alright. In the daylight his features were more pronounced; small pale blue eyes, a sharp long nose, sallow skin, the top of his head pushing through straggly hair. Tall, slightly stooped and those dreadful teeth; he was one of the ugliest white men I had ever seen. His clothes hung on him as if there was no flesh beneath. The smell from his breath strengthened my belief that he'd been eating shit. He handed me a plate of cereal. His nails were dirty and broken.

'My wallet,' I said.

He snorted.

'I need light,' I said.

He looked at me and I silently prayed that he wouldn't smile. I was sure I would throw up if he were to bare those teeth again.

'This we can do,' he muttered as he turned away.

'I need piss,' I said.

'Come.' He inclined his head towards the door. 'Next time you knock on wall. Two times for piss, three times for shit, get it?' He led me to the toilet, waited until I was finished and took me back to the room.

'I need clothes. My bag?' I tugged at my T-shirt hoping he understood.

He shook his head and locked me in once more. By the mattress, he had left a small bedside lamp with no shade and a broken neck.

Now, by the light of day, I had a better look at what was to become my prison for an indeterminable time. Shapes that I knew to be letters were scraped on the walls, but with no education, I could not read what they said. I realise now that they were the names of other unfortunates who had suffered the same fate as myself. The wall was scarred by small straight lines and rude graffiti. Scratched in the plaster, there was one sensitive drawing of a girl with a baby. Whoever had done it had a great deal of talent. The mattress was so stained that the original colour was lost and the blanket and pillow were dirty and torn.

It was then I realised what all the small lines on the wall were. They were the days marked off by each unfortunate soul held here before me and for the first time I regretted that I had not stayed with my schooling in Bangladesh. I wanted to write my name on the wall, to somehow make my mark and let others know I had been here too, that I, Abdul, had existed. I wished I could memorise the names already there in case I would someday be able to tell the world.

From then on, the only time I left the room was to visit the toilet. Food was delivered by an anonymous hand through the hole in the door, but not regularly. No one spoke. The window was nailed shut and even if I had managed to open it, I was five floors up and the ground below was a yard of broken concrete and overflowing waste bins.

By the second day, I became hysterical, screaming and kicking the door, but no one came. Finally, I gave up and sank in an exhausted heap on the floor. Footsteps passing outside never ceased, did not even hesitate, unaffected by my outbursts.

My only knowledge of passing time was the changing light through the window. From there I could see over the roofs of houses to a park, to where there were trees, green grass and flowers, swings and mothers with children. They seemed so happy out in the weak, British sunshine, totally oblivious to what was going on a short distance away from where they walked and in all probability, lived.

I spent hours peering through the hole in the door, but all that was visible was the feet and legs of those who walked up and down the corridors. Well-pressed trouser legs and shiny shoes, scruffy trainers and slimy jeans and everything in between. One day, trotting along beside them I saw skinny legs with ankle socks and small feet. Then there were the noises; swearing, shouting, sobbing, harsh laughter. I heard the grunts and groans and creaking beds from adjoining rooms; the sounds that never seemed to stop.

There was no respite in sleep. My nights were spent thrashing and sweating as I sank into the nightmare, relieved to wake up, only to realise all over again that the images in the darkest depths of the night were no worse than my waking hours.

I discovered the lamp worked and its light gave me mean respite from my misery as the sky darkened and the noises increased. The sounds of perverted pleasure and pain were a nightly occurrence and I knew I had to escape or go mad. I stood at the window staring at the ground far below. If I could somehow break the glass, if only I had a rope, I could climb down. My mind raced desperately around the items in the room. The blanket was much too short, even torn in strips and tied together it would be unlikely to hold. My eyes fell on the carpet and I wondered whether I could tear it into strips. Unlikely as it might be, it seemed to be my only hope. I began to work at one edge, trying to tear the threadbare fabric, trying to cut at it with slivers of wood broken from the hole in the door but I only managed to start a very small tear. My hands ached with the effort and eventually bled. There had to be another way. Desperately I ran my hands over the walls, tapping as I went, looking for any sign of weakness in the structure.

One wall seemed to be different than the rest – it sounded hollow. That was when I realise that one room had been partitioned to turn it into two. Why was I doing this? What good did knowing the structure of the house do? It seemed there was no means of escape. That night the clouds in the sky outside my window parted and a full moon shone into the room. No one had fed me that day and, as my stomach complained, I moved my mattress so the moon shone directly onto my face. Lying there I made believe I was fasting for Ramadan and allowed my mind to drift back across the miles and months.

*And once again I am lying on my own bedroll and the noises are the chirruping of crickets and tree frogs and the smell is of spices as Ammo prepares food for Eid.*

*It is the month of Ramadan, twenty nine days of fasting, eating only after the sun has gone down. As a young boy I have not before taken part in the fasting. This will go on until we see the first rim of the new moon. Then there is Eid. I smile in my semi-conscious world as my mind conjures up the excitement of the coming events. A few days before the first crescent of the moon is expected, Ammo prepares a paste of mud and water and spreads it on the floors and walls, outside and inside the house. Jasmine is cooking sweetmeats because there will be lots of visitors once the fasting is over. Every night we stare at the sky, willing the rim of the new moon to appear.*

*Today there is no school, no one will complain when I run to the village market which will be more alive than usual as customers buy foodstuffs in preparation for when the fasting is over. Meanwhile the girls make a paste with the henna leaves and paint it on the hands of the children. Once the rim of the new moon appears, A'isha will sweep the yard outside and the next day we will rise before dawn to wash. Then we'll dress in our new clothes. Everything has to be clean and new for Eid. After breakfast the men and boys will attend prayer in the mosque, while the women stay at home. Afterwards I will go to the special Eid fair, set up for the morning. There are toys and ice creams and food of all types for sale.*

*But there is something wrong. I am cold. I open my eyes and the spell is broken.*

Realising that I might be here for a long, long time, I shaped myself a knife from a large wooden splinter broken from the ragged edge of the hole in the door and began to make my own marks with each going down of the sun.

Through this hole in the door, which I had enlarged by this time, I saw them come and go. I sometimes saw a young person in school uniform being brought in. How many missing children had ended up in this prison, I wondered. How many parents still searched with hope in their hearts; how many would never know? I vowed that if I survived, I would find a way to uncover this scandal. At that moment I was filled with an undeniable resolve to survive at any cost. I had found another reason for making marks in the wall. One mark for every time I saw a child or young person walking past my door. I kept myself sane by committing as much as I could to memory and planning how I would, one day, expose these evil people. So I became a watcher and listener.

Yet, there were still times when I considered breaking the window and hurling myself onto hard ground below to a certain death. Looking back, the window was double glazed and I had no means to smash it, so it would have been a futile exercise. I might have simply lost the will to live as my daily marks became so numerous that they were in danger of becoming lost amongst the others – and then Anna came into my life.

As I scratched out my mark one evening, pressing deeply so that I would recognise which was mine among the others, a large lump of plaster split beneath my wooden knife, fell from the wall and shattered on the floor. I cursed, as now I had lost my marks and would have no idea how many nights I'd spent in this place. I screamed at no one, my voice loud through the unusual lull in the activities of the house. I threw the knife on the ground and slapped my forehead with the heel of my hand. In the following silence I sat cross-legged, my head between my knees in despair. Suddenly there was a tapping from behind the partition. I listened. It came again. knocked back once and waited. One answering tap. I tapped twice. Two taps came from the other side. Three times, three answering taps. Someone was there. Someone who wanted to communicate with me. A hope filled me up and I began to shake. I placed both hands and my face against the partition and breathed in dusty air. With racing heart I lifted my fist to knock again. And stopped, frozen. A door opened and shut in the other room, a man spoke and a girl's voice answered, a very young voice and the distressing noises of the night began again.

That night, as I found release in sleep despite the biting insects that shared my bed, I had a pleasant dream. I dreamed only about the old man. He smiled at me and nodded, filling me with a sense of peace. 'You will survive,' he said, then dissolved in a fine mist. Just knowing he was watching me gave me strength.

Then, in the silence of the early morning, I awoke to a scratching and tearing sound. I pressed my ear against the wall. Someone or something was working on the other side of the partition. It was more than scratching; it was as if they were trying to break through.

With renewed hope, I began to work. With my hands and wooden knife I scraped away as much of the loose plaster as I could. No one would know what I was doing. No one ever came into my room. From then on I had a mission, something to focus on and each day the hole grew bigger. I only stopped when the occupants of the house began to stir.

When I needed to go to the toilet, I pulled the mattress over and set the pillow against the hole, just in case. Hour after hour I scraped and tapped and listened. Sometimes the scraping and tapping was echoed back at me, sometimes there were voices – at those times I remained silent. Then there would be the sounds I had come to loathe. Sometimes there were only heart-wrenching sobs.

Finally I managed to hollow out a fair sized cavity, to be met by another sheet of what I know now to be plasterboard. I waited until I heard the scraping on the other side. 'Are you there?' I whispered as loud as I dared.

A small hole appeared in the obstruction and the point of a pencil worked its way through. It was removed and an eye pressed against the space left behind. 'I'm Anna,' whispered a soft voice.

For the first time in so long someone had spoken to me and the tears I thought were frozen in my heart forever, began to flow.

'I am Abdul.' I was so overcome with emotion that I could say no more.

I wiped my eyes, swallowed and found my voice again. 'Why we here?'

'We are here for sex. Men pay for us. Do they come for you? I've heard you scream.'

I snorted. Who would want to have sex with me? I was stinking, skinny, with septic sores where the bed bugs had feasted on my flesh. Then I thought of Shit-Teeth and my stomach heaved.

'I have to go,' said Anna and her eye disappeared. I heard a door open and men's voices. I stuffed my pillow over the hole and punched it in frustration, because I did not want to listen to what would happen next. That night her voice stayed with me; soft and gentle and very young. The thought of her in the next room lulled me to sleep despite the cold and the nipping bugs and the nightmares.

I dreamt that night of Bangladesh. I was in the yard, brandishing a stick, chasing the cattle around, so that they trampled the paddy stalks. Then I was gathering up the rice grains, so many they slipped through my fingers, running like gold dust. A voice came to me from the house, 'Abdul, Abdul.' A'isha rushed out and put her hand on my head. She was sobbing and calling my name, but she dissipated and slipped away from me and everything became black. As the shadows reached for me, I could still feel her touching my head and hear her voice, and the shadows melted. I started awake and the hand was still there. I looked upward and realised a hand had come through the hole in the wall. A slim, white hand with bitten nails. And someone was softly calling my name.

'Anna,' I whispered, fully awake. I grasped the fingers and pressed them to my cheek. She touched my face, my nose, my eyes and that touch filled me with energy.

After that we held hands through the hole whenever we could, each giving the other a degree of comfort.

Each day we worked the hole bigger until it grew large enough for me to see all of her face. She was beautiful; fair hair, large blue eyes that held a wealth of sorrow, perfect lips and pale skin. Because of my limited English, she spoke slowly and simply, stopping to explain words I did not understand. Bit by bit, day by day, in our stolen moments, she told me her story.

She was waiting for her boyfriend to come and take her away, she said. It seemed that her parents were drunk most of the time and had no interest in her or what she did. Then she met Saeed. He was older than her and for the first time in her life she knew what it was like to be loved. For a time she'd been happy. Saeed had offered her drugs but she had refused. She would not touch drugs or alcohol, she said. She did not want to end up like her parents. But Saeed did do drugs and when he couldn't pay his supplier, he told her that his life was in danger. She would have done anything to help him and agreed to sleep with other men for money, just until the debt was paid. Then they planned to go away together and start a new life. He had taken her to another house like this. 'One week,' he said as he left her, 'and then we'll be free, and I promise never to take drugs again.'

'Other houses?' I asked

She held up seven fingers. 'Seven, in London.' Here she became quiet and I heard no more that day.

Before she covered up the hole I had a glimpse of her room. Compared to mine it was a palace, with a bed and curtains, heavy and red, and the scent that I breathed in when I pressed my face against the hole was like manna.

The next time we spoke, she resumed her story. She had not seen Saeed since he'd left her and that had been several weeks ago. She was being forced to have sex with up to seven men a night and she never saw a penny. 'He'll come soon,' she explained, hand signals accompanying her words. 'But I'm so worried. What if he's already dead and I never get out of here? They moved me to this house a week ago – how will he know where I am?'

'We run away?' I asked, at the same time realising the impossibility of this idea. When I could, I was still trying to tear the carpet into strips. If I managed it, when I managed it, I would not leave without her.

'There is no escape. It's impossible. Even if we did, they would find us.'

And I heard desperation in her voice.

She was fourteen.

One day she reached out and touched my locket. 'What's this?' she asked.

'My mum give to me. Your mum to you?' I tried to indicate so that she would understand the question. In Bangladesh, a girl is given a necklace from her mother to keep her safe.

She began to cry. When she wiped her eyes, she rubbed her black eye make-up over her cheek.

One day she looked through the hole when I was praying. My prayers were the only thing that kept me sane. When I was finished, she asked me, 'What were you doing?'

'Pray to Allah, God.'

'Why?'

'Peace.' I wanted to tell her I would not survive if I didn't have my faith.

'Would it bring me peace?' She pointed to her chest.

In spite of my limited English, I understood and I put my thumbs up.

She shook her head. 'I am bad, bad.' She slapped her chest. 'So bad.' She pointed to her ears and shook her head. 'Even if there is a God, he won't listen.'

Somehow I understood what she meant. She felt unworthy to ask for God's help. In my heart I willed her to understand that God forgives all wrong doing. I nodded so hard my head felt loose, *he will, he will.*

Her eyes opened in question. I signalled to her to cover her head, and knelt on the floor. She copied my movements and lowered her head to the floor. I sang the Surah. (*In the name of Allah, entirely merciful, especially merciful. All praise is due to Allah, the lord of the world*)

Afterwards she said, 'That was so beautiful.'

Then she laid her head on her folded hands to indicate that she wanted to sleep.

Next morning, she looked different. The worry lines had gone from her face. I even heard her laugh for the first time.

'I slept last night,' she said, laying her head on her hands, 'in peace.'

After that, she often joined me in prayer.

# Chapter 17

Then one day there was no answering tap on the wall. No hand came through to clutch mine. No sounds came from the room behind the partition. I called her name, but there was no answer. I looked through the hole and it was blocked from the other side. This was not strange as, like me, she covered the hole when we were not communicating. For the rest of the day, I spent the time wrestling with the carpet, but only succeeded in tearing my hands. When darkness fell, I buried my face in the pillow. Anna, Anna, I cried silently. Where are you?

Another day passed; once again the light faded into darkness and there was no sign of Anna. By now I had made the hole in the door large enough to stick my head and shoulders through so that I could see up and down the corridor where the air was fresh compared to my room. Men and occasionally women of all nationalities continued to pass by, none showing any surprise at this dirty, unkempt boy with his head sticking out of a hole in a door. A young girl with a tear streaked face was brought in by a red-eyed man with grey skin who looked about fifty. Her eyes met mine as she passed, eyes full of terror, reflecting my own. Then the most massive, ugliest, blackest man I had ever seen came towards me. I could not tear my eyes from his face. One side of his head was flattened as if it had been hit by a shovel. *He* noticed me. He stopped and grinned and his grin was like that of a fat-lipped snake. 'Oooh,' he said. 'Ah didn't know there was ah boyo in there. Ah'll be seeing more oh yo, ma man.' Then he clicked his tongue and walked away. His clothes were clean, smart, he wore a heavy gold chain around his neck and his shoes shone.

That night there was a party, which was nothing new, only this time something bad happened. There was fighting, shouting, a melee outside and suddenly there were police sirens. Voices, screams, someone banging on the outside door. The door opening, more voices, shouts, curses. As I watched from the window, an ambulance drew up, someone was brought out in a stretcher, then the police drove away taking several people in handcuffs.

About an hour later I saw Anna again. I heard screaming in the hallway, men's voices and the sounds of a struggle. I stuck my head through the hole. Her face was swollen, one eye blued, there was blood on her lip. A well-dressed black man had her by the hair, a white guy with a pock-marked face whom I had not seen before held her arms behind her and they were forcing her towards the stairs. She was fighting like a tiger, kicking, struggling and trying to bite.

'Anna,' I shouted. 'Where you go?'

'I tried,' she cried. 'It was me – I phoned the police. I don't know where they're taking me. I don't want to go.'

The black man slapped her in the mouth. 'Shut up, bitch,' he growled. They half-dragged and half-carried her down the stairs.

Ignoring the splinters that pierced my skin, I wrestled with the wood around the hole in the door until I managed to tear off enough for me to wriggle my way out. The sharp edges scraped my chest and legs through the material of my clothes, but I barely noticed. I ran down the stairs after them. So intent were the men with Anna, that they were unaware of me. They pushed her out of the front door still struggling.

She looked back and her eyes locked on mine. 'Run, Abdul, escape,' she shouted as the black man yanked her hair, forced her into a car and slammed the door. The car revved up and threw deep-throated noises into the night before driving away, taking Anna with it. The two men stood on the kerb, watching it go, muttering among themselves.

Terrified and barefoot, with only the clothes I had come in, I took my chance and ran, slipping behind the men and making for the opposite lane. I had no idea where I was going and had barely enough English to get by, but anything would be better than this life. A searing pain shot from the sole of my foot and I realised I had stepped on broken glass. No longer able to put any weight on that foot, I hopped down the alley as far as I could. I had no idea where I was or what I was going to do; I only knew that I was free.

I ducked behind a large rubbish bin and pressed myself as close to the wall as possible. If there had been time I would have climbed inside and covered myself with rubbish.

Someone shouted something in English. More voices. Then the slamming of a door. The men had returned indoors. I was free. After pulling my injured foot up towards me, I tried to tug out the shards of glass embedded there. Now the blood flowed more freely. I looked around, desperate to find something with which to stem the flow. If I could get out of this place, get to where there were people maybe there would be someone, somewhere, who would help me. Slowly I began to crawl along the rough paving. The house door groaned open. I froze. Someone shouted something in English. More voices – I estimated about three or four men. Then in Bengali, 'Abdul, where are you?'

I had been missed.

I shrank against the wall, making myself as small as possible and tried to still my breathing. Steps drew nearer, then stopped. Someone cursed.

'Abdul, Come out now or it will be worse for you.'
Sounds of rummaging among the rubbish bins.

'He couldn't have gone far.'

More cursing.

My foot was bleeding badly, but I dared not move. I wrapped my arms around myself, praying that they wouldn't find me. Something soft brushed against my leg. I glanced down and found myself looking into the eyes of a rat. Through the orange glow of the street lamps he stared at me, his nose twitching. The men were coming nearer, crashing through bins, throwing black plastic bags of decaying waste aside. If only I could have changed places with that rat I would have without a moment's hesitation. Then even the rat turned away and, in a flash, had abandoned me.

The bin that hid me was thrown aside. 'Here he is.' A heavy-set Asian kicked his way through the debris of burst-bin liners. I struggled to my feet, adrenaline killing the pain from the glass. I ran. Half-running, half hopping. Across the road was the park I had seen through the window of the Hell House. If I could get there, I could lose myself among the trees and bushes. A sudden shot rang out and I realised they were shooting at me. Another shot. A bullet struck the bark of a tree and ricocheted, striking my leg and knocking it from under me. I fell down. As I stumbled to rise, a massive hand came down on my shoulder and yanked me upright. Although he could speak Bengali, by his accent, I guessed he was not from my country. Fresh blood poured from my foot and leg, staining his trousers, angering him even further.

Since I was unable to put any weight on my leg, the man dragged me back to the house, up the stairs and into the room. All three men walked in and surrounded me as I lay on the floor. I had no idea what to expect, but I guessed they would probably kill me. The Asian took the first kick, striking me in the stomach hard enough to take my breath away. From then on they took turns to punch and kick me. Everything went into slow motion and I stopped screaming. The pain somehow receded and I became detached from it in my mind. I covered my head with my arms and waited for the beating to stop.

'Aha, this is a very interesting thing,' said the Asian. I opened my eyes and he was holding my home-made, wooden knife. Sure they were going to kill me, I pleaded for one last shred of dignity.

'Take me outside. Kill me outside,' I cried. 'Don't let my last breath be in this shithole.'

'Oh we're not going to kill you,' said the Asian with an evil laugh, 'You are our mule. We need you.'

He turned the knife over in his hand. 'But I'll make sure you don't run again.' Lifting the spike high, he brought it down with the full force of his thick arm against my leg. I felt the wood crunch on my shin bone. 'Remember this lesson,' he shouted.

'Kill me, kill me then,' I screamed, longing for death.

It was only as I slipped into semi-consciousness that someone said, 'Enough,' and they left me whimpering and bleeding on the floor, with the wooden knife stuck in my leg. Time had become something else, another dimension and my body rose above pain. Then the door banged open and booted feet stepped in. I forced my eyes up the grubby denim-covered legs, to the tee-shirt with words scrawled across the front in broken white letters, to the straggly hair and unshaven chin of Shit-Teeth. He bent down and picked up my foot none too gently. No matter how bad my room smelt, how painful my injuries were, it was the stench of Shit-Teeth's breath that made me finally throw up.

Roughly he removed the wood from my leg and the glass from my foot and bandaged them both with a length of cotton. 'You no run again,' he said with a sneer, and he left me lying in my own blood and vomit, suffering the raging pain of fresh injuries. I lay curled up on the floor, blood oozing from my wounds. Cold, stiff and sore, I could feel the caked blood tighten over my wounded skin.

After that, the holes, both in the door and in the wall were boarded up, leaving only a slit in the door wide enough for a plate of food. I no longer had the option of going to the toilet. I was given a bucket which was seldom emptied. I also used the sink. Perhaps it was as well I suffered from endless diarrhoea and sickness, as once the bucket was full, I used the sink, flushing the waste a way with water from the tap. That sink became my best friend. Now I had only the cockroaches and my own excrement for company.

Night came and went and, without Anna, I had no respite for my loneliness. I became sick and could not eat and lay curled on the mattress as the pain from my leg and foot filled my world. My existence became a round of agony and night terrors. Yet into the madness of my nightmares, the features of my family with smiles on their faces would flash by. I think I had all but given up when I saw the old man again. He nodded and smiled and I felt a peace flow through me and lift me up. My cold body became warm. His garments were sparkling white like the High Imam and he brought the scent of limes and roses into the room. 'Do not worry. This will soon be over.' Then he faded away.

I remembered my recurring dream of being in a dark room and being beaten. Of people stealing my clothes, of rooms with blood everywhere. I had seen swings in a green field and white-skinned people before I knew such things existed. Now another nightmare had become reality. If my dreams were glimpses into the future as well as reliving the past, then I was not only going to survive but one day sit in a gleaming office, dressed in smart clothes, with blonde-haired secretaries who smiled at me as if I was their boss. And they liked me. That belief gave me the strength to survive. Once more I fell asleep.

*When I wake, I feel strange and hot and, above me, the ceiling spins.*

*Sleep captures me and I sink into a hot restless void. Again I am home and it is the dry season. Chandraj and I chase each other over the hot, parched ground. My mouth is sticky and I long for a drink of water and a cool breeze. Suddenly the chill wind of a British winter captures my body and I begin to shiver. I awake with a raging thirst. I pull myself to my feet and somehow reach the sink where I put my head under the tap and drink until I can drink no more. I feel hot and shivery at the same time. My leg throbs without mercy. I sit down and unwind the bandage and my leg is swollen and red. When I press on it pus comes out.*

Back in Bangladesh, while playing cricket, I fell one day, scraping my leg on a stone. The wound was deep, almost to the bone and pieces of grit clung to the torn skin. One of my friends ran for my brother, who carried me home and laid me on my bedroll. A'isha bathed the wound with boiled water. But despite her care, the cut became infected. Every day she would heat water until it bubbled and, after squeezing out the poison, she would bathe my leg until it was better. Here there was no A'isha to wash and feed me, no Ammo to fuss and worry. I was totally alone in my delirium, but if I were to survive, I knew what I had to do.

I had no access to boiled water but, using my bunched up T-shirt and water from the tap, I cleaned out the gunge as best I could. I lay down again and, as the pain and fever filled my world, I was lifted from myself. From above, I could see my body lying there, twisting and turning in the throes of fever. I watched for a beat, and then, so suddenly that it left me shaken, I was back in Bangladesh.

*It is after the monsoons have subsided, leaving the fish stranded in the fields. Some of the men from the village have built a dam and are shovelling the water into a net. I wade towards them. Above, the sky is almost white with the heat of the midday sun, the palm trees wave slowly in a soft breeze and the sound is the shouts of the workers.*

*'Abdul,' One of the men calls, because everyone for miles around knows who I am. I am the youngest son of Chanu. Others greet me as I bend to help pick up the fish. 'Where have you been? Your family are looking for you.'*

*'I'm helping gather the fish,' I say. I look up and my ammo is running towards me through the water. She is dressed in a white sari, the colour of mourning.*

*'Abdul, Abdul,' she cries as she splashes towards me. Her sari grows wet and clings to her legs. 'You must come home, eat. We have fish curry and bread. We are so happy to have you back again. Why are you stopping in the fields? Come home, come home.'*

*Suddenly I am younger and back outside our house. I breathe the hot air and bat at the flies. From indoors comes Ammo's voice scolding Jasmine for her laziness. I hear the clatter of pans, the crackle of flames beneath them and smell the strong spices of fish curry, and I remember what is happening.*

*Meena, my oldest sister is getting married and the women have been jabbering together for days as they prepare for the wedding.*

*'Go, Abdul, go and play cricket,' Ammo's throat must be sore with shouting, her arm sore with waving the serving spoon at me. Then she turns to my aunt. 'Every day he plays cricket – I fight with him to bring him home, and today – look at him, always here.' She throws up her hands.*

'Maybe he is looking forward to his own biye (wedding day),' one of my aunts says, and the others giggle at my denial. Everyone is happy, laughing. Everyone says what a fine young man Masud is, how he will make Meena very happy. My parents are pleased that this time she is satisfied and looking forward to marrying the man they have chosen for her. He is their second choice, she hadn't liked the first at all.

'Your happiness is most important to me,' Abboo had said when she'd apologised for her lack of enthusiasm. 'I am not disappointed in you.'

She has only met Masud twice, but I have overheard Meena tell her friends that from the very first look that passed between them, she knew he was special.

Ammo is fluttering about the place like a chicken, full of excitement. Meena's friends and female cousin have washed her in the pond, throwing water at each other as well as her, shrieking with laughter, chasing us away when we try to join in. A'isha is very young, but she is allowed to help with the rubbing on of oil, and to watch later as the older girls paint Meena with henna and turmeric. Being so young I'm allowed into the room. The designs they paint on are so clever I want to see how they are done.

The next day Masud's family will come to our house and present Meena with gifts; the sari in which she will be wed, jewelry, sweets and other things. They will also bring a turmeric paste and the girls will go into the room set up for the occasion.

When the males of his family come, the children will charge them money to get past. A feast has been cooked by the men and will be served outside on carpeted ground in the brightly coloured tent Abboo has erected previously.

*Finally the big day is here. Meena sits beside Masud, white-faced and beautiful. Her lips are red, her eyes outlined in black, jewels rest on her forehead and dangle from her wrists. Her nails are painted bright pink. Intricate designs decorate her hands and feet. Her sari is red with gold trims. Masud is dressed in gold and wears a red head-dress. The Imam arrives late; he had another couple to marry this morning. He takes the vows of Meena and Masud in separate rooms and then they meet, for the first time as man and wife. They sit close together on the stage, exchange yellow garlands and feed each other on sweets. Meena lowers her eyes and turns her head away, pretending to be shy, but I see a smile tremble on her lips.*

*Masud's family then present Meena with a gift of money, the Mhar.*

*I am hungry and the scent of curry tugs at my stomach. Several huge pans sit on fires in our yard and now bubble with the spiced meat the men have prepared. But it is not yet time to eat.*

*I laugh and laugh as my cousins and I steal the groom's shoes and he too laughs, although he will have to pay us to get them back. Children grow rich at a wedding.*

*Tomorrow there will be more feasting, but at the groom's house, and this time the young couple can relax and join in. Gradually the excitement will wear off and there will be tears. We have to accept that Meena will be leaving our home for ever.*

*'Do not be sad, little one,' she says to me. 'I will return for you often, and take you to stay with me in my new home for a few days at a time.'*

*The sun is blistering and my head hurts with the heat. Something is biting my leg. I am shrinking, being pulled away from Meena. Her voice is fading in the distance. My body jolts as if an electric current has passed through it. I open my eyes and look down and see only the stained blankets which cover me, and green snakes and huge cockroaches squirming up my body. They fill the air and laugh at me and suddenly every one of them has Hoss's face. I strike out mumbling and crying. Where am I? Where is Abboo, Ai'sha? I am still here, still in the Hell-House. I touch the locket. I still have the locket.*

I have no knowledge of how long I twisted and turned and cried out, I only know that no one came to help me. No doubt my screams let them know I was still alive.

Now and then I could think clearly and it was at those times that my ritual began; squeezing out the pus from my leg and washing the gash. Inside my frenzied mind, I know I had to get rid of the poison. How many days and nights passed, I cannot say. Then, one day, when I was squeezing the wound, a piece of stick came out. After that my pain became easier, my fever lessened and gradually the wound began to dry up.

But I had failed to escape. My one chance. I had lost count of how many times the sky darkened and lightened, of how many untouched plates of food came and went through the hole in the door. Then the old man appeared to me again. He had a white stick and with it he pointed down a long dark tunnel, rather like looking down a telescope backwards. At the end was a bright orange light.

'Do you recognise the light?' he asked.

I did. It was the colour of the paddy fields in my nightmares.

'What does it mean?' I asked, but he smiled and again I felt the warmth and the clean smell of his presence. He brought with him all the love and companionship that had surrounded me in my community back home and it wrapped itself about me and filled my heart with a strange joy. Then he vanished, but the feeling remained.

That morning, when I woke up, the fever had gone. I lay in silence on the narrow mattress for several more days, too weak to move. As my mind drifted between Bangladesh and this hell-hole, I studied the scarred wall, the broken door, the window that showed only sky. Mostly the sky was grey, mottled white, or faded black. Sometimes it was blue.

*It is easier now to close my eyes and drift away from my living nightmare. As if I am watching a movie played out on the ceiling, I see myself back home, running with several of my friends between the lines of washing strung from tree to tree, I hear again Ammo's voice scolding me, warning me not to touch the drying clothes, nagging me to stay out of the sun; my skin is pale, like milky coffee and that makes me special. Ammo does not want the sun to turn me dark like my brothers. I don't care. A'isha is shouting, telling me that she will not feed me again and I laugh, because I knew she will. This is the place to where I escaped in my mind. Where I can hear the mynah birds and watch the buffalos trail along the road, where I can play cricket with my friends until the sun sinks and our shadows grow long and thin. The place where I am pampered and loved.*

Later I did not know which was a dream or which was a memory that hung just outside my grasp.

# Chapter 18

If it were not for those glimpses of the past and the old man's appearances bringing hope that one day his predictions would come true, I would have given myself up to the fever and allowed myself to die.

I was aware that I had been very sick. When I had been ill in Bangladesh, my mother and sisters had bathed me with cool water, I was given tea with aromatic spices and a thin soup, which Ammo fed to me with pitta bread. 'You must eat to give you back your strength,' she had said. Therefore, although I had no appetite for the slop that came through the door, I forced it down an unwilling throat.

By contrast, here I had been left to die or live as Allah saw fit. I often wonder what Hoss would have done if he came back to find his 'mule' had died.

Then one night, the door burst open and slammed against the wall. The ugly black guy with the flattened head marched in. He was a giant, tall with massive arms, muscles straining at the material of his shirt, a thick neck and, atop it all, the gross misshapen skull.

'Ah, my man,' he said. 'Tonight you are mine.' He grinned, showing horse-like teeth.

I backed away and screamed. Once I started to scream I sank in a well of my own screaming, unable to stop.

He laughed. 'Scream all yo want, boyo. No one gonna come.'

Nevertheless I continued to yell and shout every obscenity I had ever heard. My body could no longer control the sounds.

The door opened again and Shit-Teeth hobbled in. 'No, no. Leave thees boy.' He grabbed Flattened-Head's arm. 'He is not for you. He belongs to Hoss.

Flattened-Head stepped back, withdrawing his hand. 'Aha, Hoss's boy.' He grinned again and nodded. 'You will make us lots of money.' And to my relief, he turned and left.

After they had gone, I crouched in a corner, shaking. I realised then that I was a thing, a mere piece of property, to be stored here until needed.

A few days after that, the door opened again. 'Come on,' said Shit-Teeth. 'Hoss ees coming. You need to shower.'

Hoss was coming. For the first time in so long I experienced a surge of hope. Much as I feared him, his arrival could only mean something in my life was going to change. I limped after Shit-Teeth to the bathroom; my wounds were still painful. He handed me a bar of soap and a clean towel. As I washed, the weeks of grime peeled from me like a second skin, I felt like a snake shedding its outer layer. It was good to feel clean again, but the sensation was short-lived. I had to dress in my stinking clothes.

Back in my room, Hoss was waiting, his eyes bright with anger. He stood in the middle of the filth and the smell, dressed in a smart suit, the aroma of citrus around him and merging with the stench to create a sickly, rotten-lime pocket of relief. Although I noticed that my shit-bucket had been removed, I wondered how he could bear to be in that room even for one minute. I mistakenly thought he was angry at the conditions under which I had been kept and the state of my body, surely even he would not want to see me live like this. Instead, he stepped towards me and stamped on my injured foot. The cuts made by the glass reopened and the pain shot to my teeth doubling me over.

138

'I hear you have been making trouble.' He grabbed me by the throat and slammed me against the wall. 'Listen, you little pig, do as I say or you will never live to see another day.'

'Kill me then, I don't care,' I said.

'Oh no. It will not be that easy.' He handed me my mobile. 'Only a fool would destroy a valuable property. Call your parents. Tell them you are happy in your school.'

I shook my head. I was in too much pain to speak to them coherently.

The hand around my throat tightened until I fought for air. Just as the world began to swim away, he released me enough so that I could breathe. He waited while I swallowed and coughed and came back to myself. Finally, when I could speak without croaking, he dialled the number, handed the phone to me, and said, 'Tell them you are at school and you are happy.'

Too afraid to do otherwise, I did as he asked. I did not cry this time. I had not cried for a while. I was beyond tears. At the sound of Ammo's voice my legs grew weak and Hoss had to grab me by the neck to prevent me from falling.

'I'm so glad to hear from you at last. Tell me, are you happy?'

I caught Hoss's warning glare. 'I'm happy,' I said.

'What are you learning?' Abboo had taken the phone.

'I am learning to speak English.' I could not trust my voice to remain steady, so I asked him about home and I mostly listened for the rest of our time. A'isha and Bahir had been sent to America to work in a restaurant, where they too would be safe from the revenge of the mafia. I shrivelled. Thoughts of A'isha perhaps suffering the same fate as myself were unbearable. 'But my brother will stay with her?'

'Oh yes. Bahir is a man now. He will take good care of her.'

I only hoped he would. I wanted to scream, to warn my parents of the dangers that lurked out in the world, but Hoss grabbed the phone from me. In the midst of this filth, he spoke pleasantly, his voice gentle, rising and falling like clear water over shining pebbles as he painted a picture of how well I was doing in school. As he spoke I sank to the floor and rocked to and fro, red-hot needles of pain shooting upwards from my foot.

Afterwards I wondered what Abboo and Ammo thought. I knew I sounded distant and reluctant to talk. Could it be that they believed it was my choice – that my new life had taken me from them? And that thought broke my heart most of all.

After he pocketed the phone, Hoss indicated a pair of trainers lying by the door. 'Put these on,' he said. 'We're going to Scotland.'

I had never heard of Scotland and had no idea where it was, but I was barely interested. If Hoss was taking me, it was bound to be another shit-hole.

The trainers were several sizes too big, which was just as well, as my injured foot had swollen to twice the normal size.

'I want my wallet,' I said.

'Wallet? Why do you want a wallet? I'll buy you a new wallet.'

How could I tell him it was the five taka note that was important? At least I still had the locket. I longed to touch it for reassurance, but if he saw it, he might take it.

I limped after him to the outside and stood for a minute breathing in the fresh air and allowing the breeze to caress my skin. It was still cold and I had no jacket but, right then, the bitter wind blowing up a stinking alley was the sweetest thing imaginable. I hated and feared Hoss, yet at that moment I loved him. He had taken me from the Hell-House. He had rescued me. He was my saviour.

# Chapter 19

As we walked towards the station, Hoss again told me what to say if ever I was caught by the police. 'You are an illegal immigrant,' he said. 'You will be locked up and tortured. You must tell them you had no other choice, that your parents are dead and I found you alone and rescued you and have been looking after you since you came to Britain. If you ever breathe one word of the truth, you will be responsible for their deaths.' When we reached the bus, Hoss handed me a satchel. 'For your education,' he said, and laughed.

I did not know what to think. It was too much to believe that I was really going to go to school at last. And how could I? Apart from the clothes I stood in, everything had been stolen. I knew I smelt bad, rotten. My clothes had never been washed in all that time.

'I'm not going to sit with you on the bus,' he continued. 'If you are caught today, you tell them you are travelling alone. I will come to the police station later and get you back as long as you do as I say.'

At the time I did not understand why he did not sit beside me. Later, when I realised what was in the bag, it all became clear. If I had been caught with the bag, he would deny any knowledge of what I was doing.

Hoss handed the tickets to the driver who looked at me and shook his head. 'He's not coming on my bus. He's stinking.'

'We've paid. We have tickets,' shouted Hoss.

'What about my other passengers?' said the driver. 'I can't stink out my bus.'

Hoss rummaged in his pocket and pulled out a wad of money. 'How much is it worth?'

The driver shook his head, but his eyes turned greedy as Hoss counted out the notes. 'My final offer,' said Hoss, waving the money. The driver hesitated, ran his tongue over his lips and stared at the notes. 'Get on then,' he said finally and snatched at the money Hoss passed through the tiny window.

Hoss pointed to a seat near the front. 'You sit here,' he said. 'My seat is at the back.' He tossed me a small plastic box with two sandwiches.

Hour after hour the bus trundled onward. I slept on and off, my head juddering against the window. At least it was warm in the bus, unlike the room back at the house. I woke in the dawn. Before me I saw the grainy shapes of hills reaching up until they disappeared into the clouds. A waterfall like a silver gash in the mountain raced towards us and vanished in a white froth somewhere beneath the road. As day claimed its rightful place, the clouds cleared and to either side of us were mountains topped by snow. Forests, dark against the white, stained the hillsides with jagged fir trees. Lakes threw sparkles back at the early sun. A silver ribbon of river wound its way among the hills, green fields, dark forests. Sometimes I saw a herd of deer.

From time to time we passed through grey towns brightened by baskets of flowers and stopped to pick up more passengers or let some off. These people looked at me and passed me by, no doubt thankful that there were other vacant seats to be had, as far away from this stinking piece of rubbish as possible.

We changed buses twice. At times we seemed to be high up and often a ground mist filled the valley below, the tops of fir trees rising from them, like faintly pencilled drawings. Finally we drove into a busy town where we pulled up alongside other buses and stopped. The doors sighed open and everyone began to leave. By now it was raining and the sky had turned slate-grey. Hoss rose from his seat and, as he passed me, he touched my shoulder. 'We get off here,' he said.

'Is this Scotland?' I asked.

'Yes. This is Inverness. Come with me.'

My first impression of Inverness was cold, wet and grey. The streets were grey. The buildings were grey. The sky was grey. I hunched my shoulders and lowered my head against the stabbing rain.

I followed Hoss along the street, past shop fronts with large windows. Before one of these shops he stopped and told me to wait outside. I sat shivering on the step until he returned with a carrier bag in his hand. 'Back to the bus stop,' he ordered. Once we got there, he took me into the toilets and handed me the bag. 'Change into that,' he said. Inside the bag was a T-shirt, a hooded sweat-shirt and a pair of jeans. He took my old clothes, put them into the carrier bag and handed them back to me. 'Wash them when we get there. Now we get another bus.' He led me to the bus station and into a sheltered area where he ordered me to sit on the bench and keep quiet. It was very cold and I hugged myself against the damp wind, which whispered its icy secrets through the open ends of the shelter. I swung my legs in an effort to stave off the chill that crept up my feet and calves.

'I'm hungry,' I said, as the pangs became increasingly hard to bear.

'Just shut up. Have I not bought you enough?' Hoss slapped me, hard. Two girls, sitting farther along the bench, twisted round and stared, horror on their faces.

'He's my son. I can hit him if I want.' Hoss returned their stare, his voice loud, angry. The girls looked away, faces red.

Another bus. Another journey. Lakes, mountains, castles. Even through the slanting rain, I could see the beauty of this land. The roads were narrower, the traffic less. Hoss sat several seats behind me, holding me prisoner with invisible chains.

And then the sea lay before us, as pale and grey as the sky, and a large boat sailed towards the land, black and white with a stark red funnel.

'There's the ferry now,' I heard someone say.

Ferry. Another new word. I looked again at the big ship, solid amid the soft grey surroundings, and committed the word to memory.

The bus stopped. 'That's us,' said the driver, looking at me. 'End of the line.'

As soon as we left the bus, Hoss ran his fingers through his hair, glanced around, snatched the bag from me and pushed me in front of him to the quay where people and cars were already leaving the ship. A skinny, white guy brushed passed and, without speaking, grabbed the bag from Hoss and went on to join the queue for the ferry. I expected Hoss to chase after him, get angry, snatch his bag back, but, without changing expression, he kept walking. I knew then there was something wrong, something important was in that bag and probably illegal. At the time I had no idea what it might be.

'Come on,' he said, and walked along the street.

This was a pretty town. The houses were different sizes with attractive gardens. From where we were I could see the mountains covered in forests and heather, and the sea, slightly choppy with white capped wavelets and ships lying off-shore or ploughing their way through the sound. The streets were not busy and people looked at me with soft eyes.

We went to the only Indian restaurant in this town where Hoss introduced me to the three Bangladeshi waiters and one chef who worked there.

'I own this place. You will help in the kitchen,' Hoss told me. 'Same hours as before.' There was no talk of payment.

There were fewer dishes to wash than in Brighton and on my day off, I was no longer afraid to go out. After so long in the Hell-House, I needed constant reassurance that I was free to leave in my spare time, and the fresh highland air was a gift. If I had ever been met with a locked door, I would have become hysterical. Hoss did not seem afraid that I would run away. With no money, no knowledge of the country, little English and the fear of the authorities embedded into my soul, where could I go?

My favourite place was the quay where I watched the ferries and the fishing boats come and go; where the sky was big and the ocean stretched into the horizon. People around me got on with their business, sometimes smiling or nodding at me, but I hung my head or averted my eyes. When the sun shone, the greyness dissolved, the sky and the sea turned blue, and yellow gorse, intercepted with deep greens, soft browns and soft ambers, covered the lower slopes of the mountains. Some of the peaks were still white with the remnants of snow. Flowers and trees blossomed and flourished in the damp climate. Colours were gentle here, blending into each other, not strong and vivid like back home, where the sky was an unforgiving blue highlighting the alarming, amazing green of the paddy.

It was not too bad here. I should have been happier; anything was better than being imprisoned in the Hell-House, but I felt as though I was encased in a bubble and everything and everyone else existed outside that bubble. Nothing was going to change. My hands soon became raw and painful from being so long in water, I had no money, I had no identity. I was a machine, stuck in a kitchen washing dishes and helping to prepare meals day in and day out. My future stretched before me like a long black tunnel. Hoss owned me and there would be no escape.

I once had nice hands. Long and slim and brown. But that was back in the days when I did no work, when the only callouses came from holding a cricket bat and my sister, A'isha, rubbed them with oil. These were the days when I ran in the sun on the hard baked earth and thought I was invincible.

One day, as I sat on the end of the pier, when both the firth and the town were unusually quiet and only a few boats, bobbing like corks above rocks puckered with barnacles, remained in the harbour, a new calmness descended on me. I gazed down at the clear, green sea. Pieces of weed and jellyfish hung just below the surface waving seductively in the whim of the ocean. The water swelled up the concrete sides of the pier, then it retreated, a steady pulse that drew me towards it. How easy it would be to allow myself to fall forward, the water to close over my head. It would all be over. I steeled myself for the plunge. I conjured up images of my family, Ammo, Abboo, A'isha, Bahir, my other siblings, our Imam, Jasmine and they were all smiling and opening their arms to me. I saw myself running down the track between the paddy where men, women and children were bent almost double, planting the young rice stalks. When they saw me, they straightened up and waved. 'Abdul, you have come home.'

'I'm coming,' I whispered as I allowed myself to lean further forward. One more inch and I would topple, the water would accept me, envelop me, close my eyes and my mouth and I would be home.

The drone of an engine and a loud splashing filled my ears, shattering my daydream, jerking me back to the present and reality. Before me the ferry sliced through the water. People stood at the rail, white faces rising from their muted clothing, all turned in my direction. The moment was lost. Someone would rescue me and nothing would change. Vivid memories of the man stabbing my leg with a shard of wood flashed at me and I knew Hoss was capable of much worse. Without even the courage to take my own life, I was less than nothing. Grasping my locket I pressed it to my lips and, wailing softly, I rocked backwards and forwards. Eventually I rose and trailed to the restaurant in time to face another pile of dishes.

That ferry had been my saviour, however. As time went on, with good food and adequate rest, I became stronger in my mind as well as in my body. But I felt numb, moving through each day, struggling with my growing demons in the night, my only emotion, fear. No doubt the other staff in the restaurant thought me a bit odd, but they were kind enough. Hoss shared a room with another man and he also had male friends who came and went. He was seldom around the work place and, when he was, I largely kept out of his way. One day I risked asking him if I could have my own room.

'Good idea,' he said to my surprise. 'The others are sick of you and your nightmares. And I am sick of their complaining.'

Now I dared to hope that things would get better. I had my own room. I was growing older, bigger. The other workers were kind to me. On my time off, I wandered through the town listening to conversations to improve my English. If only I could fully understand the language, it would be easier to escape. The thought of a British prison did not scare me as much as being within Hoss's power forever. Nothing could be as bad as what I had already endured. And I remembered the old man's words, *'You will come back to Bangladesh one day.'* There was a glimmer of hope on my horizon – just enough to keep me sane. But I still struggled to sleep each night. The black nightmares continued, but in my darkest moments the old man's face flashed before me with his reassuring smile, bringing me back from the brink. Every night I thought about Anna and dreamed about the touch of her hand.

# Chapter 20

It was June and the yellow broom still covered the mountainside and along the edges of the road. Where it faded, the purple of the heather grew stronger. There was a soft wind that day and the sun sparkled on the water. The tang of the ocean was warm in my nostrils and the sounds of life were all around me; the throbbing of boat engines, the cry of the seagulls, the soft accented voices to which I had grown accustomed, the hum of distant motor cars, the bark of a dog. Jelly fish hung in the waters below me and I thought of the translucent bony river-fish of Bangladesh. I closed my fists, hands red and painful, and dreaded the coming night. I never wanted to return to the kitchen and the sink. I wanted to run and just keep running. I should have obeyed that instinct, but my invisible chains held me to the man who had claimed my mind; turned me into a barely functioning zombie.

When I returned to the restaurant Hoss was in my room, packing my clothes in a holdall. Without being able to think, without being able to feel, my heart began to race and the sweat leaked from my skin.

Hoss glanced up and said, 'You are going to another of my restaurants. You're going on the night ferry.'

The air was sucked from the room and the weight of the last year rushed back at me so that my words trembled when I spoke. 'Where's that?' I asked. But my voice was so weak, I didn't think he heard.

'You will find out,' he said.

The next time I saw him, it was time to go. As well as the holdall, he gave me the satchel. One thing I had found out about Scotland was that the weather can change from one hour to the next. The soft breeze had become a gale and the shining water had become grey and angry. Huge waves crashed against the harbour wall as a summer storm swept the land. Fear from the gusting wind, from the sky with its tattered clouds dragged across a faded blue canvas, from the threatening waves that lifted the great bulk of the ship as it would a wooden toy, snaked through me. Like everything else in my life, I had no choice but to board that ferry. I had never been on such a large boat and the thought of being on all that water terrified me. But for the first time, I was alone.

For the first half hour I moved from side to side of the ship glancing over my shoulder, but no one paid any attention to me. People chatted together, read or drank at the bar. Finally I realised it was true, no one was shadowing me. I found myself a quiet corner and opened the satchel. My only knowledge of drugs came from the many films I had watched in Bangladesh and I suspected that was what was in the flat plastic bags taped between the pages of school exercise books. I was their mule, their courier. Against my will, I was breaking the law of the land. And my fear of Hoss was not as great as my fear for my immortal soul for having sinned, as taught to me under the iron hand of our Imam.

I had very little time to reflect on that because, about forty minutes into the journey, the rolling of the ferry grew worse. Forced to hold on to a rail to prevent myself being flung from one side of the boat to the other, I started to throw up. All around me, other people were also being sick in bags and containers. It was my first crossing and my most horrendous.

By the time the ferry arrived at the quayside, I was so sick I could hardly walk. When I left the vessel the ground seemed to move beneath my feet. A man from the restaurant met me, introduced himself as Rashid and grabbed the bag. A white, blue and yellow car drove slowly by and Rashid pulled me back so that we were surrounded by the other passengers.

'What is it?' I asked.

'Police,' he said.

It was the first time I had seen a police car, but Rashid was so nervous, I knew I had been right about what was in the bag.

Once the police had passed, Rashid relaxed, took me to the restaurant and told me I would be working with the tandoori oven. I was so small I could not reach right into the oven and constantly burned my hands and arms. The fact that this was a new job was no excuse. I was in a lot of pain from the burns, but what could I do? At least, away from the dish-water, my hands had time to heal. Although Hoss was far away, I had no money, little language and if I tried to escape he would be bound to find me. At least for now, I had no other choice.

After a couple of weeks, I was told I was returning to the other restaurant. Although the sea was calm this time, I still became nauseous. This time, too, a police car drove slowly along the quay. Hoss watched them and waited until they had passed before he took my bags. There was a bead of sweat running down his cheek. 'You have to go away for a while. I believe they're watching you.'

The next morning he came for me. 'You're going back to London. I won't be going with you this time, so you'd better do what you're told. Remember I know where your parents live. If you do one wrong thing, I will have their throats slit like pigs.'

Then he handed me a mobile phone. 'This is only for emergencies,' he said. 'There's no credit, but I can check on you at any time.'

My heart leapt. The thought of being on my own for all those miles and all those bus stops stirred something within me. Perhaps, just perhaps, I would have the chance to escape, give myself up to the police whatever the outcome. But my parents – did Hoss really have friends in Bangladesh who would carry out his orders? If only I could remember Bahir's number, and if only I had money for the phone I could warn them, ask their advice.

As it turned out, the thought of escape was no more than a fanciful dream. When I boarded the bus in Inverness, a wasted-looking youth boarded at the same time. He was a stranger to me, but I saw him talk briefly to Hoss. He did not look at me or speak to me, but sat several seats behind me and I knew he was another spy. When the bus stopped on the border, he left for a smoke and, as he passed me, he dropped a plastic carrier bag on my lap. Inside was a sealed packet of sandwiches and a can of coke. I slumped against the inner bus wall, my slight flaring of spirit already dead.

# Chapter 21

A small, thin man of mixed race with rat eyes and a long narrow nose met me in London and snatched the bag as soon as I left the bus. Without giving me his name, he walked me to a cafe where a well-dressed black man was waiting.

Without either introducing himself, or offering any conversation, Well-Dressed took me to a flat not unlike the one my so-called uncle and aunt lived in. This one was dirty and smelt terrible though not nearly as bad as the Hell-House. Nothing could ever be as bad as that house. In the middle of the room was a massage table. In one corner, sat a television. A fat brown-skinned man with a strange accent, a light skinned Asian who spoke Bangla to me with a Pakistani accent, and a thin-faced, sallow-skinned teenager sat around a scarred dining-table, packing drugs into sachets. A girl sat on the couch doing a line of coke. She had straggly fair hair, pale skin, black circles round her eyes, sunken cheeks and red nostrils. When she opened her mouth I could see gaps where some of her teeth should be. She gave me a wan smile. I asked for something to eat and she handed me a packet of crisps.

Well-Dressed left me there.

Once the men had finished packing the drugs, they all did lines of coke and drank vodka. I shrank in the corner as the party became more rowdy and the two men began to fondle the girl at the same time. One of them, in my head I called him Fat-Guy, ordered her to remove her clothes which she did. I have never seen anyone so thin as that girl. Every rib was visible. Her breasts hung like small empty pockets. Fat-Guy stripped naked and began to have sex with her. Her eyes were glazed and she offered no resistance.

Desperate to get away from what was happening before my eyes, I left the living area and looked around the flat until I found a room with three beds. I climbed into one and wrapped the pillow around my head to block out the sounds.

The next morning the girl made me coffee and toast. From time to time she gave me a small smile but did not speak. When the men rose, they began to fill my satchel with the drugs. Somehow they did not scare me anywhere as much as Hoss. I had no way of knowing what the British system did to drug smugglers and I did not want to find out. Whatever it was, it had to be a lot worse than being charged with illegal entry. Summoning up all my courage, I looked them all in the eye in turn. 'I'm not taking drugs back to Scotland,' I said. They all laughed and carried on packing. The girl began to prepare a line of coke on the coffee table.

'I mean it,' I said. 'I'm not doing this anymore. I'm going. I'm leaving. If you try to stop me I'll call the police.' Filled with a new determination, I held up my mobile phone. During the previous night, as I tossed and turned, I spoke to Abboo in my mind. He was a good, just man, and he stood up for what he believed no matter what the consequences. I was sure he would expect the same from me. If I had been able to speak to him, to ask his advice, I knew what the answer would be. 'If it is against the law of Islam, do not do it. If you die for your beliefs, then it is the will of Allah.'

I had to take this chance. Straightening my shoulders and feeling braver than I had in a long time, I turned to walk out of the door. I did not know where I intended to go, or what I was going to do. I was still desperately afraid of both my captors and the police, but somewhere in the hours of darkness, a new determination had flared within me and given me the strength to stand up for what I knew to be right.

The Pakistani shot from his chair and grabbed me. Small and slight as I was, I fought like a madman to be free, slipped from his grasp and grabbed the door knob. Then Fat-Guy's hands were on me. 'Why not, boy,' he said, spinning me round and slamming me against the wall.

'I don't want to any more. It is against our religion.' I met the Pakistani's eyes. 'We are both Muslim. Our law says that we must treat each other with respect and kindness. Why are you doing this?'

'Religion doesn't put food in my belly,' he said in Bangla.

Fat-Guy bent my arm backwards until I felt it was going to break. They picked me up and threw me on the massage table.

I yelled and thrashed about.

Fat-Guy seized both my arms, Thin-boy held my feet until my struggles became useless.

'If you are going to kill me just kill me. But I will not carry your drugs anymore,' I shouted.

'Oh no, we won't kill you, but we will make you suffer,' said the Pakistani, and he stuffed a rag in my mouth. The beat of my heart grew loud in my ears and I thought I was going to suffocate.

For a short time he disappeared and returned with a pair of bolt-cutters.

Fat-Guy grabbed my wrist and pinned it to the table. 'This'll remind you who the boss man is,' he said.

The girl started to scream.

Pakistani slapped her. 'Shut up, bitch.'

Her screams muted to snuffling sobs.

Fat-Guy held my wrist.

Pakistani came towards me with the bolt cutters.

He placed the blades around my little finger and

squeezed.

The pain burst up my arm, multiplying until I dissolved and my world was a red haze of nothing.

When I woke up I was still on the table. Sharp stabs of red-hot pain shot up the length of my arm. My hand hung over the side of the table, as heavy as lead. When I tried to raise it, the weight pulled me over and I landed on the floor. It was then I saw the stump of what had been my finger, swollen three times its size, black and burnt.

The girl was sitting on the settee injecting something into her thigh. The young white guy was playing a TV game. Both turned to look at me writhing on the floor but neither rose to help me. My tongue stuck to the roof of my mouth. My hand and arm were on fire. My throat was bursting. I kept saying, 'panna', the Bangla word for water.

'What is he saying?' TV-Guy looked at the girl. She shrugged her shoulders.

I kept crying and calling out for panna. Finally he rose to his feet and grabbed the phone. Only then did I realise how young he was, probably not much older than me, white-faced and sunken eyed.

He shouted into the receiver. 'He's awake. He keeps saying panna. What does he want?'

After he hung up, he brought me a glass of water, helped me to my feet, led me to another room and onto a bed where I drifted in and out of consciousness for a time.

Eventually there was no respite in oblivion. My world was filled with screaming agony.

The door opened and TV-Guy came in and handed me two tablets and a glass of water. 'Here, this'll help the pain.' His hand shook so much that the water slopped over the sides of the glass.

I didn't want to take the pills as I had no idea what they were, but I was in so much agony I would have done anything. Ten minutes after taking them, I forgot my pain. I forgot everything. The room was filled with bright colours and I was floating on air. For about four days I was in hallucinatory state. When I came back to myself, I had little memory of how long I had been here. The room was stinking with vomit and every other bodily fluid. I could only remember screaming and trying to climb walls. The pain in my finger was much less and my mouth felt like cork. I only wanted to drink and drink and never stop.

Fat-Guy had returned. He came into the room and looked at the mess. 'You fucking filthy bastard,' he yelled, and he smacked me hard, knocking me to the floor. 'There's a fucking toilet through there and you shit on the floor. You fucking animal. Get this cleaned up.' And he kicked me.

I lay there, among my own filth, nursing the pain from his boot and my finger, laughing hysterically.

'Get this shit cleaned up, now,' he said, and slammed out of the door.

After I managed to control the laughter, I rose and went to the toilet. When I returned the girl was there with a bucket and mop and a roll of kitchen tissue. 'I'll help you,' she said.

Once we finished, TV-Guy brought me sandwiches and water. I realise now that he was concerned and frightened, but young, afraid and addicted. Neither he nor the girl could do anything to help me. They, too, were victims.

Two days later, a big white guy with massive shoulders, a bald head and several tattoos arrived. Everyone seemed afraid of him. He gave me a new pair of trainers, a T-shirt, jeans and a hoodie and told me I was going back to Inverness. 'If you ever feel like doing anything stupid again, look at your finger. It will be worse next time.' He nodded towards my crotch. 'You could be rich and comfortable or mutilated and dead. Your choice.' Then he stared into my eyes. 'Get this into your head – the one thing you'll never be is free.' He handed me the satchel.

Yet another Asian got on the bus behind me and as he passed me, he dropped a sandwich on my lap, then, just like the others, he sat at the back.

I was very tired. I'd had no natural sleep for a week. Each time I drifted away, the throbbing in my finger brought my dilemma sharply into focus again and I would start awake, sometimes with a scream. It was a journey of discomfort, pain and desperation. The driver must have been relieved to reach his destination and be rid of me.

Yet another nameless man met me at Inverness station. Pasty-skinned with a massive stomach, he grabbed my arm. 'Are ye Abdul?' he said. His voice was low and gravelly.

I nodded.

He handed me a ticket. 'Gie that tae the driver,' he muttered, pointing to the correct bus, then he walked away. Another dark-skinned man boarded the bus. He did not look at me and I did not know whether he had been sent to watch me, or if he was just an innocent passenger. Not that I cared. I was beyond caring.

We reached the port just as the ferry docked. When I got off the bus Hoss was waiting and the first thing he did was to grab the bag. He glared at me with black anger. 'Why are you giving trouble to people? I know all about it.'

The routine had become familiar. The skinny youth came along wearing a hoodie and low slung jeans. He grabbed the bag and joined the queue for the ferry.

As we walked down the street, Hoss told me I was going to work in a restaurant in a town on an island for a while and I was to stay quiet. Once inside my room he grabbed me by the throat and squeezed, his fingers digging into the sides of my neck. 'Don't ever try to make trouble again,' he said, his face so close to mine that I felt his spittle on my cheek, smelt his aftershave and tobacco breath. Then he picked up my hand, looked at the stump of a finger, still black, blistered and swollen, and he laughed. 'Hurts does it?' I heard the threat in his words. 'Believe me, I can do much worse.'

The restaurant on the island became my home for a couple of months. I learned more about cooking there and got on well with the staff. Along with them, I was once more moved to practice my religion which gave me a tremendous amount of comfort.

Then, to my distress, Hoss brought me back to the mainland. The trips between London and Scotland began again. Although my finger healed, my memories did not. I never argued, no longer having the will to try. I caught what little sleep I could between nightmares and work. I was a nothing. A thing to be used. To be controlled. Less than human. I only spoke to answer a direct question and did as I was bid.

Eventually, I guess Hoss was satisfied that he had broken my spirit enough to trust me to do the trips unsupervised. He gave me pocket money, just enough for food on the journeys. Before every trip he instructed me on what I had to tell the police if I was ever caught. And always the threat of what he would do to me and my family if I got him into trouble hung over my head.

Struggling to smile always, I gave the appearance of accepting this as my role in life. I tried not to think of home. I didn't care what happened to me anymore.

If ever a rebellious notion crept into my mind, I would look at the stump of my finger and remember the big man's threatening stare at my groin. Yet, when I touched the locket my ammo had given me, something deep within me failed to accept that I would never be free. Someday, I believed I would, although I could not see how. I knew of nowhere I could go that they wouldn't find me. I had no money except for the little Hoss gave me, I had very little English and knew no one apart from Hoss's friends.

After a successful trip, Hoss was nice to me and rewarded me with presents. He might buy me a jacket, or some new trainers. Once he bought me a watch.

The nightmares grew worse. Now added to the mix was the vision of the bolt-cutters closing round my finger and of my parents dead bodies covered in blood should Hoss ever carry out his threat. I struggled through every day doing what I had to and collapsed into bed at night with nothing to look forward to but another struggle with my demons.

My body desperately craved sleep. One night after I returned from a trip, I fell into bed and immediately drifted away. I can't say how long I slept, but I woke up to find Hoss naked in bed with me, his hand stroking my private parts. With a yell, I twisted around and beat my fists against his chest.

'Enough of this,' he said with a snarl. 'You belong to me. You will do as I say when I say it.' With one arm he held me against him, the other hand roamed my powerless body.

I continued to struggle and scream. By now I was good at screaming.

'Be quiet or you'll be sorry,' He put his hand on my mouth but someone had already heard and came into the room.

'What are you doing?' shouted a waiter.

'Nothing, get out,' Hoss said, his voice low and menacing, but the waiter did not move.

'Leave the boy alone,' he said. 'I warn you…'

'*You* warn *me*?' Hoss rose, grabbed the waiter's arm and pushed him into the corridor. Outside my door the angry voices rose then fell. Thankfully Hoss did not return.

I had been reprieved this time, but the others in the restaurant were also afraid of Hoss and I knew they could not continue to protect me. A few might be here illegally and to make trouble for Hoss would mean making trouble for themselves. Terrified, I snuck to the kitchen and helped myself to a carving knife. Back in my bed, I held that knife so tightly that the blade sliced into my hand. I was determined to kill Hoss or myself if he tried to force his perverted lusts on me again. Although I had locked my door, I knew that he could get in if he really wanted to. With my heart thundering in my ears, my body limp with fatigue, my stomach threatening to empty itself, and the blood running freely from my hand, I drifted into a semi-conscious state.

# Chapter 22

I was startled into wakefulness by a pounding at the door. My first thought was that Hoss had returned. I leapt out of bed and poised with the knife raised. A voice shouted, 'Police, open up.' I trusted nothing and no one now. I did not know whether this was the British police or another one of Hoss's stunts. I only hoped the lock would hold.

Then came the sound of breaking glass and two uniformed figures burst in through the window. When I saw their white skin and uniforms, I realised this really was the British police; that one way or another I was going to escape Hoss's clutches. Lowering the knife I smiled in relief. In my heart I was thankful for this intervention, no matter what it might lead to.

They backed away. 'He's got a knife,' one said. I realised at that moment how I must have looked, standing there, covered in blood, clutching a knife and grinning like an idiot, the sheet trailing behind me, stuck to my body by dried blood. I flung the knife from me and held up my hands the way I'd seen it done in the movies. One of the policemen leapt forward, yanked my arms down, twisted them behind my back and hurled me face down on the bed. I thought my arms were going to be dragged from their sockets. Straddling me, he handcuffed me and tightened the cuffs until they stopped my circulation. The pain was unbearable.

A pretty, blonde policewoman came in with a dog. 'We've got them all,' she said, and then her voice rose, 'What are you doing? That's just a kid.'

The officer stood up and yanked me to my feet. 'So?' he said and shrugged his shoulders. 'He's one of them.'

The dog was wound-up, running round the room sniffing and yelping.

I was manhandled out of the bedroom and made to stand against a wall with the others including Hoss. I was in so much pain from the cuffs I was crying out loud.

'What's wrong?' said the policewoman and came over to me.

Turning me round she looked at my hands and shook her head as if in disgust. From her pocket she took a key and loosened the cuffs. As she did so she noticed the stump of my finger and she started back; her eyes opened wide. 'What happened to your finger?'

Hoss shot me a warning glance and answered for me. 'He doesn't speak English. He was chopping meat with a cleaver. Accidents happen.'

The woman said nothing but a faint wash of colour climbed over her cheeks and the shock remained in her eyes.

'Why did you have a knife in your bedroom?' she asked me more gently.

'I was afraid,' I replied, not looking at Hoss. This was my chance to tell the truth yet terror stilled my tongue. In any case, my English wasn't good enough.

'Afraid of what?' asked the policewoman.

Again Hoss answered quickly. 'He has nothing to be afraid of. He self-harms. We've been doing our best to stop him, but...' He shrugged his shoulders.

The policewoman looked at me and something in her eyes told me she did not believe this story. Here was a complete stranger whose job it was to arrest me and throw me in prison, one of the enemy, yet her presence filled me with a tentative hope.

They kept us standing there until midday. As the drug squad did a thorough search of the premises, the police phoned immigration. Because of the strange accent in this land and the speed at which they spoke, it was impossible for me to follow what was being said. Eventually the officers came back into the room. They spoke for a long time, glancing occasionally at me, nodding or shaking their heads. I had no idea what was going to happen. My legs and feet had gone numb from standing in one position. Only the wall behind me kept me upright.

It was therefore a relief when they moved us again. They roughly bundled us into the back of a van where it was dark and stuffy. The door slammed and the blackness was complete. The engine growled into life and the van did a quick U-turn which threw us against each other. With our hands behind our backs, it was difficult to manoeuvre ourselves back into position. Again and again, we struggled to maintain our balance as the vehicle sped along the twisting roads.

As we travelled, Hoss schooled me once more on what I had to tell the police. He repeated the story as he had so many times throughout the years that it was embedded in my mind. That he had treated me kindly, that I had never had to work, that I had only been in the UK for a year, that I wanted to come back to live with him. That my parents were dead. He bombarded me with horror stories about what would happen to my family if I ever told about the drugs, the girls or the boys; Hoss's tastes were very diverse.  We were all warned and re-warned not to mention any of it. I did not reply. I was afraid for my family, but more than that, I knew I couldn't tolerate any more. I was drained and empty with no life and no self-respect and I would happily go to prison if it meant Hoss would be brought to justice and my parents kept safe.  My gorge threatened to rise with every bend and at last I vomited over my legs, and, with a certain degree of satisfaction, over Hoss's.

They took us to the police station in a pretty village. A white and glass building amongst the grey. When my turn came to be checked in, the officer asked me my name and date of birth. I did not know my age; I had been ten years old when I left Bangladesh, but had no real way of knowing how long I had been in this country. Days had melted into weeks, weeks into months, months into years. I stated my name, then shrugged my shoulders and shook my head.

'Take him away,' said the officer. 'We'll deal with him later.'

Two officers took me to another room where they searched me, removed my shoes and took me to a cell. It was like walking into a fridge. A fridge with a narrow bed, no blanket, a metal toilet without a lid and no window.

The officer closed the door and as he turned the key in the lock, it made a grating sound that vibrated in my head. Memories of the locked door and the scarred wall of the Hell-House were too fresh and, holding on to my self-control with every ounce of my strength, I huddled in a corner, my heart beating wildly. After a while a man came in and gave me a plate of fish and chips which were barely warm and soggy. I ate most of them, both hunger and nausea fighting for supremacy.

I was kept there the rest of the day. As the cold crept into my bones I sat, staring at the blank wall, my body rocking with a jerking motion, my breath coming in gasps, pin-pricks of terror filling me up. I struggled against the panic, consoling myself with the thought that Hoss was suffering the same fate and that whatever happened to me, at least I was safe from him.

But no matter how hard I tried to hold on, the dread rose until it had me in its grip. I had to get out of here. I could not stand the locked doors, the tramping feet outside, the shouts from my colleagues in adjoining cells. Someone was crying, great wracking sobs. They too believed the horror stories Hoss had spun of a British prison, or perhaps their fear of being sent home to a certain death was even greater. We all had our own reasons for panic. Eventually my control slipped and crumbled, I threw myself around the cell, crying out, crashing into the walls, kicking the door. The metal door. No one came. It was hopeless.

'You're not in the Hell-House, you're not there, you're not there,' I repeated the words as if hearing them aloud would give me strength, my voice rising as images of the worst time in my life re-emerged. My words reached a crescendo and I began to bang my head against the door repeatedly. As I collapsed shivering in a corner listening to the shouts and cries of the other terrified prisoners, I spoke to myself. 'You fool. You thought you would be better off in a British prison. Now look at you. Idiot.' The laughter bubbled up and burst out of my mouth.

The shutter in the door slid open and a pair of blue eyes peered through. A female voice said something but I wasn't listening. By that stage, I was hysterical. Like a crazy person, laughter and tears had taken me over.

The woman went away and came back with another officer. They came into the cell and she spoke to me in a soothing voice, asking me what was wrong. I continued to shake and laugh pressing my teeth together, fighting for restraint but finding none. Taking my hand, she led me to the bed and sat down beside me. If it had not been for the memory of the other hand, Anna's hand, and the comfort it had brought me, I might have fought her off. Now I sat, clinging to that hand, still giggling and shaking, my heart beating like the wings of a wild bird trapped in a cage.

'Abdul,' she said, 'My name is Simone.'

'Get away from him,' said the other officer. 'You're putting yourself in danger. He looks mad.'

'He's a child,' she snapped. A lot more words followed, angry words that I could not catch.

Eventually the other officer shrugged. 'Have it your way,' he said, and slammed out of the cell.

Simone stayed with me for at least an hour until I had settled down. All the time she talked in a calm, kind voice. Then her radio went and she rose. 'Excuse me,' she said. 'I have to go. But don't worry, you're safe now. You'll be alright. Trust me.'

Once again I remembered the words of the old man and I did trust her. But I didn't want her to go. She was so kind and I wanted to go on listening to her soothing words although I hardly understood their meaning. I was still confused but I believe her compassion brought me back from the edge of insanity that night. Why she didn't notice that I was shivering and needed a blanket, I don't know. Perhaps in Scotland they'd grown so accustomed to the cold that they didn't notice it, I thought.

Sudden exhaustion hit me like a sledge-hammer and, in spite of everything, I fell into a state of oblivion. As I slept, I dreamed again about the old man and I saw him sitting on a chair that wasn't there, smiling and radiating a sense of calm. Suddenly I was surrounded by the scent of roses and limes and I wasn't cold anymore.

'What's going to happen to me?' I asked. 'How long must I stay here?' He didn't speak, but he looked happy and from then on I sensed his presence like a warm glow enveloping me, bringing me peace. I believed it was just a matter of staying calm, of waiting. Next morning the cold was through me and my limbs were stiff and sore bringing yet more painful flashbacks of the Hell-House. I opened my eyes and looked at the bare walls, the steel toilet and the steel door. From another cell someone was crying aloud. Slow footsteps sounded along the corridors outside. I closed my eyes and pressed my forehead against the wall, hoping against hope that they would come and get me soon; I couldn't stand another day in this place.

The door opened and an officer came in. 'Eat up, you're getting out of here today.' He brought me cereal and a drink of water and he smiled at me.

'Where I go?' I asked.

He shrugged. 'Wherever it is, it'll be better than this.'

His words filled me with a glimmer of hope and gave me an appetite for my breakfast. After I had finished, the officer returned and took me into another room with chairs and a desk. A well dressed, dark-skinned man was waiting there. He stepped forward and offered me his hand. At first I shrank back, wondering whether Hoss had sent another of his men for me.

'Abdul,' he said. 'I am Kassim. I am your translator.' He was very well spoken, like a doctor or a lawyer. I let out a rush of air I'd been holding tight inside. He indicated that I should take a seat in a vacant chair. It was good I had a translator because there were many words I still didn't understand, especially in this land where the accent was so different from England. He told me that he had already spoken to Hoss and the others. I was the last.

Simone and the officer from the day before came in and I could hear the anger in her voice as she shouted at her partner, her words too fast for me to catch. Her face was red and her nostril flared slightly with each outbreath. The way the pair kept glancing at me told me that I was the cause of the argument. I caught the words, "children's home."

Kassim translated. 'She is very angry that you were kept in a cell. She says you are a child and should have been put in a children's home.'

'A…a children's home?' I asked.

'A place for children who cannot be with their families.'

'I want to go home. Tell them I want to go back to Bangladesh.'

'Listen to me. Forget about your parents. Bangladesh is not safe for you. Think only about yourself. You are safe here, in a good place – you must not worry. There is a better life for you here. The authorities will care for you until you are eighteen. If you still want to return to

Bangladesh then, no one can stop you. Do you understand?' He stared at me.

'Am I going to prison?' I asked. That fear still haunted me.

'No. You will not be going to prison. '

'Are you sure?' Hoss's stories were deeply ingrained.

'Listen to me. I would not lie to you. You will be safer here. Trust me; I'm doing what is best for you.'

Something about him made me believe him. He was right. Bangladesh was not safe for me. I was sent here to flee from Kamal and his gang and their memories were long. 'Think only about yourself,' Kassim said.

I didn't know what to do. In spite of the cold, I began to sweat. I could not tell the truth. For my parents' sake, I had to stick to Hoss's version. Even if he was locked up, he had many contacts.

Kassim then explained that I had to be examined by a doctor. 'We have to find out how old you are,' he said.

He spoke some more to Simone and she smiled at me. 'You're going to be fine now,' she said, the tone of her voice calming me a little.

'They are bringing a doctor in to see you. Normally you would go to a hospital to be examined, but they feel you might not be safe there,' explained Kassim.

'Why are hospitals not safe in this country?' I asked.

'They are afraid you will escape or be abducted. In the meantime we will get you something to eat and drink.'

'I won't escape. I don't want to escape.'

'You must do what you are told for now.'

It was another hour before the doctor came – a woman with a sour face. She slammed her bag on the floor; I had the feeling she was not having a very good day. She looked at me without speaking, grabbed my hands and sucked some air between her teeth. Then she told me to take off my clothes. I shook my head; I didn't want to stand naked in front of a woman. Thankfully, Kassim caught my look of silent appeal. As a fellow Muslim, I was sure he would understand.

'I'll leave the room if that makes you more comfortable,' he said. 'But you must be examined. She is a doctor. She sees lots of naked bodies. Men and women. Yours will mean nothing to her.'

His leaving didn't make me feel any less embarrassed, but I did as I was asked and slowly peeled off my clothes, covering my private nakedness with my hands. The doctor gave me a thorough and humiliating examination and, as I dressed, she smiled at me for the first time. 'I will sort everything for you,' she said, 'I'm pleased to have met you.' She shook my hand and left.

Again time stretched. The tick of the clock on the wall sounded extra loud. Officers came and went, but Kassim remained with me. Then another woman came into the room. She said nothing, but nodded at me then turned and said a few words to Kassim and they shook hands.

They spoke for a few minutes before Kassim turned to me again. 'It appears you are thirteen or fourteen at most,' he said. He indicated the new woman. 'This is Mrs Mackie, a social worker.'

'What's a social worker?' I asked

He explained that a social worker was like a manager who would look after my interests and since I was so young, she had to be here when I was interviewed.

I was questioned at some length by the police, Kassim translating, talking quickly.

By now I was tired and, unable to sit still, I tapped my foot on the ground, twisted my hands together or rubbed my neck. I glanced often out of the window where a tree dipped lazily and scratched at the glass. No one reprimanded me. Whatever happened next, I would have to accept it. Again the words came at me, what will happen, will happen. The voices in the room floated around my head, making little sense as they spoke quickly and quietly. Sometimes one of them would leave and return a short time later.

Then Kassim told me that I was going to a children's home. The social worker wanted to take me with her there and then, but the police would not allow it. For my own safety, he said, they were going to escort me to my new home themselves.

'Will I be locked in?' I asked in horror, dreading the thought of the cell – another locked door. I knew I couldn't survive it. I rubbed the knuckles of one hand so hard against the other that it hurt.

He shook his head. 'No. You will be well looked after. Didn't I tell you?'

'Where – what's going to happen?'

'That's not for me to decide. When you are eighteen you can do what you want. The man you call Hoss wants to take you back to with him.'

The room swum before me. The images blurred. My body went cold, yet sweat prickled my armpits. This was the worst news I could have heard. 'But... but isn't he in prison?' I asked.

'They had to let him go. They found no drugs anywhere other than in your room and by law they cannot hold him.'

'But there were drugs...' My slight flare of hope crashed around me. I couldn't believe I was hearing this.

'I know what happened. But Hoss was the one who tipped off the police. I think he is very cunning. There was a party the night before and a white girl claims to have been molested. She had been very drunk and cannot identify her attacker. Hoss knew there was going to be trouble, so he made sure the premises were clean, then he reported it to the police as if he was innocent and his employees were doing stuff behind his back. He would have known that you would be taken into the care of the authorities and, being so young, would not be sent to prison. No doubt he believed that you would be returned to him if he claimed to be your legal guardian.'

I went quiet and stared at the ground, my breath quickening. 'He would have been the one to have molested her. The others would not do that. He is a very bad guy,' I said. 'He has hurt a lot of people.' Hoss free. He could get to my parents, get to me. I would never be safe. My hands bunched into painful fists. Now I could never tell the truth.

'Don't worry about him. Do whatever you must do to remain safe.'

'But the police have to do something.' How could this be true? How could Hoss still be free?

'Without evidence, they can do nothing, but don't worry,' Kassim said. 'They take care of children in this country.'

My voice disappeared, my shaking increased. The feeling of helplessness overwhelmed me. How could I only think of myself? I had to do whatever it took to protect my family even if that meant returning to Hoss.

Outside, the sun shone from a clear blue sky. The breeze blew softly against my face carrying with it the scent of the sea. Birds wheeled and cried above our heads and distant traffic had become a steady hum from the main road. Once again we travelled by car, through streets with paintings on the walls of the buildings and flowers in baskets hanging outside houses and blossoming in gardens. We drove through a lane with high hedges on either side and came eventually to a large modern building.

There people were waiting outside the door. Adults and happy-looking kids. A bunch of girls and one boy. They greeted me as I left the car and shook my hand. Inside the building, I was given a plate of sandwiches and shown to a room with pink walls, a bed and wardrobe and a chest of drawers. There were curtains on the window.

'This is your room,' said Kassim.

Looking back, it seemed to be a girl's room. Perhaps she had been moved so that there was a place for me.

A woman came in with a towel, pyjamas and a dressing gown over her arm. 'I am Margaret. Come away, son. You need a bath. Then we'll find you some new clothes.' She had kind eyes and a gentle voice.

After my shower I lay on the bed too exhausted to move and I had never been in such a soft bed. I imagined sinking into a cloud. The quilt puffed up around me, even the air smelt sweet. Now that the excitement had died down and I was comfortable, warm and fed, I became more aware of the injuries caused by the rough handling I had received at the hands of the arresting officers, the self-inflicted bruises when I threw myself around the cell in panic and my chafed, dish-water hands. Feeling safer than I had since leaving Bangladesh, I allowed sleep to overcome me. For the first time in so long, I slept without dreaming. I slept until nine-thirty in the morning. When I rose, the police, Kassim and the social worker were all waiting for me. They had arrived at nine o'clock but had not wanted to disturb me. They had only come to see how I was. This overwhelming show of concern unnerved me; everything was so different from what Hoss had led me to believe would happen if the British authorities ever caught me. Still, I was unsure; confused. At any minute things could change. I fingered the locket that had never left my neck since Bangladesh. The locket I held for comfort every night. *What will happen will happen, it is your fate.* The words spun in my head.

After breakfast, Margaret gave me a complete set of new clothes. As I dressed I watched myself in the mirror and, although I was thin, I looked like any other kid.

A knock came to the door. I was still nervous and jumped slightly as it opened. A very pretty girl with soft brown curls and green eyes carrying a small jar in her hand entered and sat beside me.

'I'm Chardonnay,' she said pointing to herself.

'Abdul,' I replied setting the flat of my hand against my chest.

'I know.' She unscrewed the lid from the jar, took one of my hands in hers and began to apply the cream. 'They will soon heal here.'

Chardonnay became my close companion and I still remember her fondly. I loved it in that home; the other kids liked me and everyone seemed to care. After my recent experiences, it was the nearest thing to paradise on earth.

Then, a week later, the police returned. I was playing basketball with the other children when two police cars turned into the drive. A shiver ran the length of my spine and I knew something was wrong. In spite of everything they had promised, I had an underlying fear that I might, after all, be returned to Hoss.

I held the basketball in my hands and I stopped, frozen, staring.

A policewoman and another officer left the car and came towards me.

Time slowed. It was a hot day and a haze shimmered between us.

The sound of my heartbeat filled my ears and I felt my pulse in my neck and the top of my head. I counted the number of breaths it took for the officers to reach the playground.

The woman's mouth opened. 'Abdul, all of you come on, now,' she ordered. 'Get into the building.'

A few kids moved slowly, confused. Others stood where they were. My feet were rooted to the ground.

'Quickly now. Move!' The officer's voice rose.

As if suddenly overcome by a communal fear, our eyes flew all around, feet pounded the ground as we raced inside. Once we were indoors, the policewoman whispered to Margaret, who immediately locked the door and shouted to the other staff to come to the office.

'Go to your room, Abdul,' Margaret said. 'The rest of you follow me.'

I looked out of the window. Another two officers stood outside the home. Something was happening – something bad.

Then I was called to the phone. It was Kassim. 'Pack your bag. You are not safe there anymore. They are taking you away.' He explained that Hoss wanted me back. He was arguing with the police, threatening to take them to court. Other guys phoned the station too, saying they were relations and would take care of me. If I stayed in this home, he said, there were real fears that Hoss would find out where I was and snatch me back.

All that night two police cars sat outside my window. I thought that they were guarding me in case I ran away. I laughed to myself. If only they knew, running from them was the last thing on my mind.

Next morning my social worker, Kassim and two officers arrived early.

'They are going to move you somewhere else, where no one will find you,' explained Kassim. He shook my hand and wished me luck.

'Will I see you again?' I felt panic at the thought of losing this man with whom I had already begun to form a bond.

'I can't say, but remember what I said. Think only of yourself.'

'Where am I going?'

Kassim shook his head. 'Even I do not know that,' he said. 'They don't know who told Hoss where you were, and now they trust no one.'

One of the staff came in, packed my bag for me and gave me yet another change of clothes and shoes. She wished me good luck. As I left, everyone stood on the doorstep and waved. Chardonnay had tears in her eyes.

I remembered leaving Uncle's flat in London and how no one had said goodbye, how no one had seemed to care.

# Chapter 23

The sun shone that day, dancing on the sea, throwing sparkling pebbles of light towards me. Now and then we drove through shady forests with the tallest trees I had ever seen and the light, broken by the leaves, peppered the ground. We drove past a large loch, flat and still. We drove on mountain roads, where the land lay far below in patches of colour, browns, greens and astonishing yellow. The policewoman sat beside me and offered me sweets. It had been so long since I had been shown such kindness, my heart was bursting. I closed my eyes and the sun warmed my face and made dancing patterns on my eyelids.

The policewoman touched my hand. 'Everything that happened to you,' she said gently, 'it's all been for a reason. Fate brought you here.'

A smile warmed its way across my face as I recalled the words of the old man.

I could feel him at that moment. He was with me in spirit wrapping me in invisible arms. In spite of that, I was almost scared to believe my ordeal was finally over. Surely Hoss would not harm my parents as long as I stuck to the story he had drilled into me over the years. He could not blame me if the authorities would not let me go back to him. I prayed silently that they never would.

'Will I be safe?' I asked.

'You are going to the safest place on earth,' she replied. And I had the strong sense of having come in a circle. I had left a happy life in Bangladesh in the summer sun and now I was leaving the worst time in my life, again under a clear sunny sky.

'What's it called?' I asked. 'This place you're taking me to.'

'It's just a small town. The name isn't important right now.'

Yet another new name – another new place. We drove through small pretty towns, past lochs, waterfalls and castles. Finally we came to a town and drove down tree lined streets until we pulled up outside a low, white building with large windows. Directly across from it was a green field with swings.

'We're here,' said the policewoman. The driver went to the door to announce our arrival. It was flung open by a young man with a wide grin and black curling hair. By then I was out of the car and standing on the pavement, my case beside me. The young man came over, shook my hand, introduced himself as Peter and greeted me in my own language. *Great* I thought, someone to communicate with me fluently.

'I'm so happy to meet you. Where did you learn my language?' I asked.

He raised his hands and shook his head. I realised then that he only knew how to say 'hello' and 'welcome'. He had been expecting me and had been learning some words in Bengali just for me.

I was in a foreign land, far from my own culture and family, still struggling with the language, still unable to read or write, but at that moment I was the happiest boy on earth. Among good people, I would one day be free to tell my story and somehow make a difference. And Hoss – even although Muslims are instructed not to seek revenge, I knew I could never be at peace as long as he had not paid for the crimes he'd committed.

# Chapter 24

Peter led me and the police officers to the office where I was introduced to Bill, who was to be my social worker, Kathy, the manageress, and another four women. I was surprised that a woman would be in charge over the men. This was unheard of in Bangladesh.

I sat on a chair and caught snatches of their conversation as they discussed what to do with me. One of the women left and brought me a drink and a sandwich and the discussion continued. Never having been in this situation before, as I found out later, they didn't know what to do with me. I gathered that I would have to go to the police station to have my fingerprints taken again.

'Come on,' said Peter finally. 'I'll show you your room.' He led me down a corridor. I did not feel so comfortable here; the atmosphere was heavy, the corridor stark. We passed a spacious room with a pool table and dart board and table tennis. Inside a fight was going on between two teenage boys. Others were shouting and swearing. One of the by-standers turned and looked at us as we passed the open door. His eyes met mine and there was so much anger there that it darkened the space between us. It was as if everything I had suffered was encapsulated in that boy's eyes and I shrank inside my own body until I became nothing more than a tight knot. I shuddered and wished myself back in the first home.

Peter opened the door to a room. 'This is yours,' he said.

There was a television, bed, wardrobe and chest of drawers. The window was high up. Although it was a nice room, to me it felt like a prison.

Peter's next words strengthened that feeling. 'You are not to leave the building,' he said very slowly so that I understood. 'You will be watched at all times. I'll leave you to get settled in. And,' he paused and looked at me. I nodded to let him know that I got his meaning. 'We'll do our best to see you are happy here.' Still shaken by the hatred in the boy's eyes and the sense of danger carried with it, I sat on the bed, chewing on skin around my nails until I drew blood.

At dinner time I was taken to the dining room. Silence fell as the other kids turned to stare at me with hard eyes. Six boys and two girls who looked even tougher than the boys. 'Fucking paki,' one whispered. 'They've put a fucking paki in with us.' Unseen by the staff, she leaned towards me, spat in my food then picked up my fork and mixed it in. The others laughed.

'No, I'm from Bangladesh,' I said, wilting under the violence that shimmered in the air around them.

'No difference. You're all the same,' said the boy who had glared at me earlier. He was much larger and broader than me with close cropped hair, a flat nose and thick lips. He jabbed at his chest with a finger. 'I'm Dillon. And you are dead.' I have since heard that, a few years later, he died in a police cell.

Someone kicked me under the table. 'We're going to kill you,' another kid said with a grin.

I said nothing and avoided looking directly at anyone as the hissing and insults continued in low voices. When any of the staff came in, everyone fell silent.

'Not hungry, Abdul?' asked Peter. I was, but could not stomach the contents of that plate. I shook my head and studied my hands, one folded over the other to still the tremble.

Then Peter escorted me back to my room. As he turned to leave, he paused and looked at me. 'Keep the door locked at night. It's safer.'

After he had gone, I turned the key in the lock. Although my fear of being imprisoned persisted, the fact that I held the means to open that door made all the difference. I sat on the bed and switched the television on, to discover there were only five channels and they were all in English.

It was as well I was locked in. About half an hour later someone banged at the door. Booted feet crashed against the wood. 'Open up, fucking paki.' It sounded like one of the girls.

'What's going on?' an adult voice shouted, a voice of authority. Then there was muted laughter and footsteps running away, silence for a beat, then loud music from the room next door. From down the hall another television was blaring. Then it came again, swearing and whispered voices outside my door.

The banging at the door resumed. 'Open up, you black bastard,' shouted someone. By now I was curled in a corner hugging myself as tightly as I could as the knocking escalated to kicking and someone throwing themselves against the door which seemed to bulge inward, straining at the lock. My breath was now noisy gasps, my heartbeat racing as I pressed myself against the wall, sharp sobs of fear rising in my throat. Then a woman's voice. 'What's going on here? Get back to your rooms.'

'Fuck off,' said someone.

'Do you want me to get the police again?' She was obviously not afraid of them.

More mutterings and shouted swear words as the footsteps of my would-be assailants echoed down the hallway.

I was not disturbed again that night, yet, in spite of the fact that a few yards from me was a bed with blankets, I remained huddled in my corner, cold, trembling and too scared to move.

The next day Kathy came for me. 'We're moving you to another room. This home is really not the place for you.

The kids we have in right now are a real bad bunch.' She took me to the kitchen and gave me breakfast. Cereal and toast with tea. 'Don't worry about a thing, we're all here to protect you. From now on, you'll eat with the staff.' She said a lot more, but I could only get the gist of her words.

I rose and began to wash the dishes. 'No, no, said Kathy. You don't have to do that.'

'I must help,' I said, confused that I was being waited on.

She looked at my hands which were almost healed. 'You don't want dish-water hands do you?'

Remembering the state my hands were once in, I almost laughed. 'But I must work, mustn't I?'

Peter rose from where he sat at the table and took a pair of yellow rubber gloves from under the sink. 'Wear these,' he said, 'And if you work we'll pay you.'

'I can make tea, too.' I was surprised that I would be earning some money I could actually keep. From then on I made the tea for the staff and was known affectionately as chi-talla (tea-boy).

On the second day, the social workers and police came to see me again, with a local doctor who originated from Bangladesh, to translate.

'Where is Kassim?' I asked.

'He lives too far away,' said the policeman.

The doctor spoke to me for a while, but he was from another region and his dialect was different to mine. Still, I could communicate better with him than I could in English. He found out what I liked to eat and what I most needed. I was surprised that the staff were so concerned about my welfare. This was a new experience. After the bland food I had been eating, I yearned for a good curry. I asked him if I could practice my own religion, and he said he would see that it was arranged. Since there was no mosque in this town, I was allowed special times of the day when the staff made sure that I was left in peace for my prayers.

Food was not a problem.

'I can cook for myself,' I said, seeing the confused face of the cook as she studied the list of spices I had requested.

'Sure,' said Kathy, looking relieved.

That night I cooked a curry to the surprise and delight of the staff. I liked them all and in spite of the language barrier I enjoyed my time with them and our limited conversation.

I only had one change of clothes, so a complete outfit was bought for me, jeans, trainers, jacket, T-shirts, underpants and socks. All this, and I was not even expected to work.

But where the grownups were kind, whenever they saw me, the other kids threatened me, spat at me or backed away, saying things like, 'Yeuk,' or 'black bastard'.' Even the girls didn't like me. One was big and very heavy with studs in her eyebrows and lip. Her name was Sheree. The other was Lyn, thin but broad-set and wore her hair cropped close to her head. Her eyes were constantly angry. The girls seemed to hate each other, yet sometimes they shared cigarettes, or pooled their money to buy cheap wine which they drank in the field across from the centre then smashed the bottle on the road.

That night a massive fight broke out between a couple of the boys which led to a near riot with the others taking sides and the police had to be brought in. The shouting and anger filling the building terrified me so that I shrank against the wall, like a quivering mouse. I could not understand why those kids, with all the advantages that this country offered them, even within the walls of this centre, would deliberately want this trouble. Why were they not grateful?

Later, I overheard Peter say to Kathy, 'Get Abdul out of here. This is no place for him.'

For a long time I was kept as far as possible away from the others and there was always an adult with me. In the main sitting room was a TV with satellite channels. Every child was allowed half an hour a night to watch a program of their choice. When it was time for my half hour, all the others were put out of the room and a member of staff stayed with me.

That night Kathy sat with me. 'I have to go to the toilet,' she said after a bit. 'I won't be long.'

The minute she left the room, Dillon came in and punched me on the mouth and head. Then he put his face close to mine. 'You tell and you're dead.' His spittle landed on my face.

When Kathy returned she ran to me. 'Who did this?'

My lip was already beginning to swell, blood poured from my nose. Something about Dillon reminded me of Hoss; his swagger, his way of manipulating the others. I was too afraid to say anything so I shrugged and stared at the ground. Sometimes a poor understanding of English came in handy.

# Chapter 25

The biggest fear for my future was that I would somehow be sent back to Hoss. I knew this centre was not forever, that I would have to leave eventually and Hoss was still out there, still wanting to control me, still owning me, still holding the power of life and death over my parents. I could not tell anyone how much I hated and feared him. And yet, I had been his puppet for so long, I could not shake off the invisible pull of his chains. I was left with no will of my own, so I continued with the lie that I wanted to live with him and he had been kind to me, while praying that they would keep me from him.

In this place I was relatively safe; there were adults looking out for me, I was in a better situation than I had been for a long time, yet my nightmares grew worse. Now they came every night; the dark shadows in the fields, the stench of the Hell-House, the beatings, people stealing my clothes, monsters coming at me with wire cutters, cutting off my fingers. Flashes of horror, intercepted by the smiling face of the old man and the blonde girls. There was always so much noise from the other rooms – TV's blaring, boys shouting through the walls at each other, that my cries in the night were never noticed. Even in my waking hours I suffered flashbacks and I would begin to shake, my heart rate would speed up, beads of sweat would blot my skin and I would long to be able to hide in a corner. I would clasp my locket in my hand, and draw strength from the memory of my ammo placing it around my neck. Each day I was so tired from lack of sleep that my feet felt like lead and my head ached. Yet I smiled and thanked my protectors and hid my pain in a well deep within me. What more could they do for me?

One morning a lady from immigration came to see me with the doctor who had originated from Bangladesh to explain what was going to happen next.

'You'll stay here for now. You're the first case like this we've had in the Highland Region and no one knows what to do with you. The authorities feel you'd be in danger both in Bangladesh and with Mr Hossain in Britain. We do our best to protect children under eighteen.'

I thought of the young people I had seen being brought into the Hell-House and wondered how effective their efforts were.

'They'll get you a solicitor who will sort your immigration details. We do not have the expertise here.' The doctor explained that they were considering sending me to Glasgow because they felt my needs would be better met there.

The interpreter went on to say that the law in Britain stated that I had to have an education and that a meeting was being held to decide how that was going to happen, given that I could not read or write even in my own language.

I listened to everything I was told, angry at the lies that both Hoss and 'Uncle' had told my parents about the cost of education. Now I was being told it was not only free but compulsory.

Two days later they brought in a lovely lady who introduced herself as Moira. 'I'm a teacher,' she said. 'I'm going to help you with your English.'

I was keen to learn and she came in every day for the entire summer break from school.

Meantime, some of the other kids in the home were getting uncontrollable and I was constantly in danger of being beaten up. Some of them would have liked me, I'm sure, were it not for Dillon. They were only nasty when he was around. Once when Dillon had gone home for the weekend, he returned to find some of the other kids watching TV with me. He swore and shouted at them, and threatened to beat them up. They were all afraid of him.

A week later I was called to Glasgow to speak with my solicitor and to see about my immigration status. When the time came to go, I was surprised to find Kathy, the manager of the home, John, Allan and another social worker all waiting to transport me. I laughed at the security; there was no chance of me running away. However difficult it was in the home with the other kids, these people were trying to protect me from Hoss and I needed that.

I had been assigned Kassim, who had been my interpreter in Inverness for the Glasgow interview.

When we walked into the solicitor's office I was worried, but full of hope. I would have been happy to be sent back to Bangladesh to see my parents again. Perhaps at that time I would have told the truth. My nervousness increased as the need to blurt it all out grew in me.

The solicitor smiled. 'Nice to meet you Abdul,' she said. 'We have brought in an interpreter. This is Kassim.'

At first I was happy to see him.

Kassim sat in front of her desk and he half turned to face me, nodded and grinned. 'How are you? You look well. The lawyer has to make a case to present to immigration for you to stay in this country,' he said in Syhlet. But something was wrong. He looked unsure and constantly rubbed his palms together.

'Will they send me back?' I asked.

'If they think you are in danger and your parents are dead, the government will let you stay. If they send you back and harm comes to you there, they can be sued. They won't risk that. Once you're eighteen you can do as you like.'

He rubbed a hand across his forehead. 'But you won't return, will you, Abdul? You will go back to Hoss. You have to. You belong to him.'

My skin crawled. My stomach somersaulted. I glanced at the other faces in the room with panic and I was suddenly glad of all the security. This man I had trusted had turned on me. Hoss couldn't get to me here, could he?

'How are you a friend of Hoss's?' I stammered before my voice gave way.

'How many Bangladesh translators who talk Syhlet do you think there are in Scotland? Four – that's how many. Hoss can get to any one of them. You cannot hide.'

I never knew I could feel so hot and so cold at the same time. My palpitations began again and my palms grew wet. I rubbed them on my jeans. 'But you said I had to think of myself…'

Kassim looked at the floor. 'I am thinking of you, and of your parents.'

'Does he understand what I'm saying?' asked the solicitor, looking worried.

'He understands,' said Kassim in English. He turned to me and spoke in Syhlet. 'When it is time to go, tell them you need the toilet. Tell them you want me to come with you. Then we are getting out of here.'

I shook my head.

'If you don't, Hoss will see that your parents are killed, you know that. They are only alive because you've kept quiet so far. The minute you make trouble for him you have signed their death warrant. He's very powerful, you can't hide. Have you stuck to the story like he told you?'

I didn't know what to do. My mouth was dry. I would die myself rather than go back to Hoss. My understanding of English had greatly improved but speaking it was a lot harder. My brain was reeling. When the interview ended, I said nothing.

Lowering my head, I stared at the ground so as not to meet Kassim's eyes. Everyone stood up.

'He told me he needs the toilet,' said Kassim. 'Wants me to come with him.' I knew by the edge in his voice he was angry that I had not obeyed him by asking myself.

'Is that right, Abdul?' asked John.

I stared at him, trying to tell him the truth with my eyes and nodded.

'Away you go then,' he said.

Kassim walked with me to the toilet. My legs felt as if they would not hold me. This could not be the end of my hopes and dreams. I looked over my shoulder and saw John several paces behind. He winked at me. John knew I could speak enough English to have asked for the toilet myself. Surely he would guess that something was wrong.

As soon as we entered the toilets, Kassim fished in his pocket and pulled out a phone. 'I've someone here who wants to talk to you.' He dialled a number and handed the phone to me.

'Abdul, you fucking little shit.' Hoss's voice, the voice I hoped never to hear again, hit me with the force of a sledge hammer. 'You've lost me a pile of money. You get back here and pay me my money back.'

'What money?' I stammered.

'I've lost everything because of you. The police took everything I had. Tell them you want to come back to me if you want your parents to remain alive.'

'I have told them I want to come back. I've done everything you said. They ... they won't let me go.'

'Then run away.'

'I... I can't. They ... watch me all the time.'

'Is there a window in that toilet?'

I glanced up. There was but it was very small. Just at that moment John knocked at the door. 'Are you all right in there?' My mouth was so dry I could not speak. My head began to throb.

Kassim opened the door enough to tell him I was still in the toilet.

I rang off, slid the phone in my pocket and slipped sideways so that I caught John's eye through the slightly open doorway.

'Come on we have to get going,' he said.

I pushed my way passed Kassim and the phone rang.

'What's that? Where did you get a phone?' said John. 'Give it here.'

I pulled it from my pocket.

Kassim snatched it out of my hand. 'It's my phone,' he said. 'Abdul wanted to make a phone call.'

'He's not allowed,' said John, glowering at Kassim.

John shouted something and the social worker joined us. They began arguing with Kassim, voices rising and talking so quickly I couldn't catch what they were saying. John turned around and shouted to Allan, 'Phone the police.'

Kassim grabbed me, pushed me roughly aside and said in Bangla, 'Hoss knows where you are now. He will phone you at the centre on Saturday. Be there.'

'Come on.' John ushered me out of the building to where his car sat in the drive, the others followed, pushed me inside and John started the engine. Allan and the other social worker sat on either side of me each with an arm extended across me, as if they expected me to try and break free. If only they knew. If I had been hit in the stomach with a cricket bat I could not have felt so ill. At that moment a police car pulled up. Two police officers jumped out. Kathy spoke to them for a minute, then climbed in beside John. 'Just drive, get out of here,' she commanded.

The wheels squealed as they gripped the tarmac and we sped along the road and onto the motorway.

'That was Hoss. He called me.' I said, my voice shaking.

'We know,' said John.

Kathy held a hurried discussion with the others in the car and then made a phone call.

'We've to go straight back,' she said after she'd hung up. 'They say it might not be safe to stay away overnight.' It was already late in the day and it was three in the morning by the time we reached the children's centre.

'Don't think I can cope with this,' said Kathy. 'Put the coffee on someone – although I could do with something a lot stronger.'

John made a sandwich and I was allowed to sit with them to eat. 'He... Hoss is going to phone here on Saturday,' I said.

The next morning the police came and spoke to me, just to see if I was alright. Their concern still amazed me. Why should these people in this strange land be so bothered about the welfare of a worthless illegal immigrant?

I smiled and thanked them and told them I was fine, but that was far from the truth. I was terrified. They had no idea of the lengths Hoss would go to to get me back. He must have threatened Kassim to make him change so drastically. At that time I believed he would have my protectors killed if they stood in his way. I did not know then that he was too clever for that. Even he would not risk killing a UK national – not because he had any conscience, but because that would bring the full force of the British law system on his head.

Bill came one day and spoke to Moira, my English teacher. 'Authorities say Abdul must go to school. They are setting up a place in the High School.'

Moira appeared shocked. 'You can't put him to High School. He can't read or write. He's coming on, but he can barely write his name. He needs to go back to the beginning. Put him to primary school.'

'We can't put a boy his age in primary school.'

'Than let me help him until he catches up.'

'They won't have it. You were only employed for five weeks. His English is pretty good now and they won't continue to hand out money for a private tutor.'

'I'll do it for nothing. He's coming on so well. I don't want to leave him at this stage.'

'I'm sorry. I agree with you but the decision is out of our hands. He's got to go to secondary school.'

That Saturday, the police set up the means to record the conversation when Hoss phoned. When the call came, Hoss was told it was not possible to speak to me. I don't know what was said, but the staff appeared nervous afterwards.

'If ever you see him,' the police officer said, 'get someone to phone us right away and we will set up road blocks.'

'He's found you. He's hired a lawyer to fight for custody of you. Now we might have to move you after all.' John looked me in the eye. 'You don't really want to go back to him, do you?'

I shivered, the longing to tell John the truth filling me up and making my eyes burn.

'Yes – he was good to me,' I said. But I shook my head as I spoke, the lie trembling on my lips. No matter how much I wanted be honest, I couldn't, ever.

John sighed. 'Well, son, we can't let you go to him. We believe you'll be in danger.'

He studied my face as the relief flowed through me.

'We're still thinking about sending you to a home in Glasgow. It will take a wee while to organise. Don't worry, you'll be well protected. In the meantime, you have to go to school.'

I had to trust them. I believed that they were doing the best for me, but Hoss was an evil man and his invisible restraints still bound me, his threats still terrified me and the degree of brain-washing I had been subjected to, forced me to constantly deny that he had harmed me in any way. The things I knew, I could never tell, at least as long as Hoss was out there. My fear was worse now that I knew he'd found me.

My nightmares leaked more and more into my daily life. The loud voices and anger of the other boys and the bullying tactics against me brought me out in sweats, yet I smiled my practised smile. I was so grateful to the staff for all the kindness they showed to me.

One day some boys tried to interfere sexually with a girl. I shrank in the corner shaking and crying, all the horror of what had happened in the Hell-House swamping me. When my legs were strong enough to hold me, I ran to find Kathy. Then I locked myself in my room and curled up beneath my bed.

# Chapter 26

After the incident, Bill sat and spoke to me for a while, then said, 'You've been stuck in here too long. It's time you went out. Come on.'

I was thrilled. It was good to be away from the home, to be able to walk around town for the first time, to be free from the taunts of Dillon and his friends, to be outside the confines of the centre and the constant supervision. Bill took me through the streets, to the harbour where the fishing boats were moored and reflected in the still water, the marina with its small yachts and unsteady walkways, the cafes and fish and chip shop. Trundling lorries drove past and an old man with wizened face looked up at me from his boat moored along the pier wall. 'You like the boats, son?' he asked me as I studied the nets and coils of rope on board.

I nodded. 'I like small ones. We had boats in Bangladesh.'

'Bangladesh, eh? Would you like to have a sail in mine sometime?'

'Yes, thank you very much.' I wasn't sure. The water within the harbour looked safe enough, but I still had memories of the ferry ride to Lewis.

Bill took me by the river, along the path between trees that shadowed the ground, where dappled pebbles of sunlight fell through the leaves and shafted and shimmered in the distance. Birds filled the air with their songs.

Then we went along the main street, a small town street, nothing like the thoroughfares of London, nothing like the busy holiday atmosphere of Brighton, similar but different to the slow pace of life here. This town had its own tempo, a heartbeat belonging to it alone. Bill pointed out the shops for clothes and the supermarkets for food. Then he told me that I was going to see the school that night. And as we walked I calmed down and my mood lifted.

Back in the home, still full of the elation of that walk, I passed another kid in the hallway, and I said, 'I'm going to school soon.'

'Fucking school. Why would you want to do that, mongo?' His fist arched and came down hard on my stomach. The pain doubled me for a second, but at that moment I didn't care. He must have thought I was crazy when I laughed. He imagined he had hurt me, if only he knew what real pain was.

Nothing dampened my spirits for the rest of that day. I was finally going to get the education my parents had wished for me. I longed so much to talk to them, but even if I had a phone, I would not have known how to reach them. Some of the numbers still clung in the recesses of my mind, but they were jumbled and spun away before I could trap them or put them in order.

That evening, Bill took me to a large, grey building with high, narrow windows and elaborate stonework. A well-dressed man met us at the door with a smile. His hair and eyes were as dark as mine, but his skin was pale in comparison.

'I'm the headmaster.' He shook my hand firmly. 'I'm going to show you around.' His voice was strong and deep. Instinctively, I trusted him.

'Is school open at night?' I asked.

'I'm the headmaster. If I say it's open, then it's open.' He lifted up his hands and laughed after he said the words.

He took me all round the building; showed me the classrooms, the canteen, the hall for dancing, the PE departments. Compared to the school in Bangladesh, it was like a palace. I was so excited. I was actually going to get an education. I would meet other kids who had to be better than the ones in the home. I would make friends. A surge of joy filled me up and I wanted to jump and laugh. As it was, I smiled. All the way round that school, I smiled so much my cheeks grew tired. I was sure I would do well here and I was over the top enthusiastic about starting school in two days' time, after the summer break.

'Of course you'll not be attending classes right away. You'll go to the Base until you catch up. But while you are here, if there is anything you want, or if you have any problems, come and see me.' The headmaster went on to explain that the Base was where they taught kids with learning problems.

'We'll have to get you all things you need, lad,' said Bill as we walked through the streets towards the centre.

'I need clothes. I've saved a hundred pounds from the money you paid me for washing dishes.'

'You don't need to use that. Every kid gets forty pounds a week for clothes. You have over three hundred pounds in your account.'

I was completely taken aback. 'Who from?'

'The government. Come on, lad.' He set his hand on my shoulder. 'Tomorrow we'll go out and cruise.'

The following day, after the early meal, I collected my savings and went down town. As we walked, he told me he had a son my age and he had a good idea what clothes boys liked to wear. We bought pencils, clothes, toiletries and hair gel. He took me to have my hair cut. 'Someday soon,' he said, 'I'll introduce you to my son.'

When the first day of school finally came, I rose early, dressed in my new clothes and gelled my hair. I turned both ways, admiring myself in the mirror, and then an abrupt fear gripped me and I began to shake. The home had become a refuge; the thought of suddenly being without the support of one of the staff or a social worker left me cold. My high spirits deserted me and I felt myself plunge into a deep, dark hole filled with terror. Out there was the shadow, out there was Hoss.

Bill found me sitting quaking on the bed. 'Come away, Abdul, you're going to be late.'

My fists bunched the bedcover at either side of me. 'I... can't go.'

He sat beside me and put a hand on my shoulder. 'What's up, lad? It'll be fine. I'll stay with you all day.'

I shook my head. 'I can't go,' I repeated, more loudly this time. Beads of sweat rose on my skin.

'Then let's just go for half a day, see how you get on, okay?'

I swallowed. My head had begun to throb.

Bill rubbed my shoulder. 'Just half a day. We can do it.'

It was the use of the word 'we' that gave me strength. He would be with me. I nodded, but felt sick.

The air was fresh and clear that morning. It had been raining in the night and everything smelt brand new and, as we walked, the fear gentled and was replaced by a surge of bravado. I could do this. I had to.

As soon as I entered the school the bravado deserted me and I became an alien. Everywhere we went, the other kids stopped what they were doing and stared at Bill and me. I could feel their eyes on my back as we entered the headmaster's office and again when we walked to the Base. Once inside the Base, I looked around in horror. This was a place for kids with learning disabilities, or who were behind for some reason and the majority of the pupils attending that morning could do little more than colour pictures. Many of them coloured in pictures or played with building bricks. Boys and girls, all in together.

'What am I doing here?' I asked. 'Why can't I go back to Moira?'

'I don't make the decisions,' Bill said. 'It'll get better.'

'But I don't want to stay.'

Bill rubbed my shoulder. 'Give it a try, please, for me?'

A very nice lady teacher came over, introduced herself. 'Tomorrow'll be better. You'll be in with kids like yourself who are behind for one reason or another.' She gave me a book. 'For today, perhaps you'd like something to read.'

'Tell her I can't read,' I hissed to Bill.

The lady's face reddened. 'Oh, I'm sorry. Of course.' She returned with some crayons and paper. 'Would you like to draw?'

I was upset that I had embarrassed her so I said, 'Thank you very much,' but inside I felt frustrated. I had come to school to sit and colour in like a little child.

After she had gone, I turned to Bill. 'I think I'm in the wrong place. What am I going to learn here? I don't want to colour pictures.'

'You just need to settle,' Bill explained. 'It takes time.'

After a while, the head master came into the room and sat beside me. 'How are you getting on?'

'I don't want to be here,' I said. 'I'm learning nothing.'

'There's a PE class on in a minute. I'll take you to that. I'm sure you'll like that better.'

'What's PE?'

'Physical Education. Remember, I showed you the hall last night. You'll see.'

When he led us into the PE hall, all the other kids stopped as if suddenly frozen and stared at me. Some were standing around the wall, others were hitting what looked like a bunch of feathers with a bat.

'Come on in, Abdul,' said the PE teacher. She stepped forwards and gave me her hand. 'I am Ms Nichol. We're playing badminton. Would you like to try?'

It looked like fun. I nodded.

'Give me your racquet, Joe,' Ms Nichol shouted and the boy called Joe tossed it to her. She handed it to me. 'See that net? You hit this shuttlecock to the boy at the other side.' She held up the bunch of feathers. They were attached to something like a half-round. A shuttlecock. Another new word.

I held the bat for a second testing the weight, then I threw the shuttlecock into the air and hit it with the racquet. I watched as it flew across the room. My opponent swiped at it and it came back towards me. I hit it again and laughed. This was indeed fun. I forgot the staring eyes, I forgot to be nervous, I forgot everything except the thrill of the game. After a while, Ms Nicol stopped the game. 'Well done.' She clapped her hands. A few of the kids clapped tentatively as if it were expected of them.

The teacher's smile was wide. 'Oh, we definitely have a new champion,' she said to the class, 'What do you think of our chances in the matches this year?'

The kids looked uncertain. Ms Nichol turned to Bill. 'We run a badminton club on a Thursday night. Abdul's a natural. I want to see how well he does in a proper game.'

'Would you like that?' asked Bill.

I definitely would. For the rest of the session, I watched the other kids playing and took mental notes as Ms Nichol explained the rules.

After the class was over, I didn't want to return to the Base and asked Bill to take me home. The head teacher stopped us on the way out and asked if I was okay.

'Yes thank you. But I can't learn anything in the Base.'

'It won't be all the classes,' he explained. 'And only until you can read and write.'

'You did well,' said Bill. 'Tomorrow, how about trying for a full day?'

I said nothing. I wasn't at all sure.

The next day, the headmaster was waiting for me on the front step. 'Today, I'm taking you to registration.'

'I've got to leave,' said Bill. 'But you'll be fine.'

The panic began to rise in me.

Bill must have noticed my face. 'Just stay calm. I'll be back at lunch time.'

I rubbed my hands down the sides of my jeans and over my hair, and walked with the Headmaster down the corridor to a classroom where he opened the door and indicated that I was to step inside.

'Hello, class,' he said, 'I have a new pupil for you. This is Abdul. I know you'll all look after him and make him welcome.'

'Hello, Abdul,' said the teacher. She was young and pretty with a gentle smile. 'Just go find yourself a seat.'

All the desks had two children sitting at them. The boys immediately spread out to either end of the bench so that there was no room for me. One boy was sitting alone. A big, broad lad, he had red hair, pale blue eyes and his face was a mass of freckles. He too started sliding from side to side of the bench as I drew near, leaving me no room.

'Oh dear,' said the teacher, 'It seems as if no one wants to sit with you.'

Two very pretty girls sat in the front row. One of them stuck up her hand. 'Please miss he can sit with us.' With her fingers, she flicked her long black hair over her shoulder and as it settled, it rippled and shone. When she smiled at me her deep blue eyes sparkled and a jolt of something shot through me, drying my mouth. She moved up to make room for me. Some of the others giggled.

'No, Kirsty,' the teacher said, then to me, 'Don't sit with these girls. I'm always giving them detention. They'll get you into trouble. Hamish, let him sit with you.'

The big boy who sat on his own scowled, but moved along the bench. I ran the gauntlet of the staring eyes, took my seat and set my things on the desk. The teacher and the headmaster went outside the door for a minute presumably to discuss me. As soon as they left, a titter ran around the class. 'Poor Hamish,' someone hooted, pointing at us. Several boys began to throw paper balls and rubbers at Hamish. His face turned red and with one angry movement, he swept all my things off the desk, scattering them over the floor.

Kirsty shot to her feet, came over and picked up my things. 'Don't be such a dick-head, Hamish.' She set my stuff back on the desk and beamed at me before returning to her own seat. Her eyes crinkled at the corners when she smiled and her cheeks pinked. Hamish, his face turning scarlet, his mouth pursed, kicked me hard under the desk.

The teacher returned. 'Everything alright, Abdul?'

Nursing the pain in my leg, I nodded and said nothing.

Once registration was over, I followed the others into the hallway. Kirsty took my arm. 'I'll show you to your next class.' I caught Hamish staring at us, a look of pure hatred on his face.

'Never mind him,' Kirsty said. 'He fancies his chances with me himself. Perv.' Fancies, dick-head and perv were words that I did not know, but I didn't want to appear stupid, so I smiled at her and said, 'Thank you.' It seemed I had at least one champion in this alien world.

'You know, there is a school disco on Saturday. You have to come.'

'Disco?'

'Dancing,' she said. 'Come with me. I'll show you.'

'I won't be allowed. But thank you very much.'

The next class was geography. No one would sit beside me and again Kirsty was made to sit in the front row beside her friend. She flicked her hair and glanced back at me over her shoulder, treating me to another of her smiles. A smile that lifted my heart. At least in this room there was a vacant seat where I could sit alone without bothering the others.

'Does anyone know what a monsoon is?' asked the teacher. A few tentative hands rose, but mine shot up.

'Yes, Abdul,' said the teacher.

All eyes turned to me. Some of the boys laughed.

'He knows nothing,' Hamish said. 'He's a Baser.' Then they stared at me expectantly as if waiting for me to make a fool of myself.

I explained exactly what a monsoon was. I had lived through too many. As I spoke I was back there under the gushing water, like a waterfall pouring from the sky, filling the streets so that they ran like rivers, turning the paddy fields into muddy swamps.

The teacher was delighted. 'This is great. So good to have someone who was actually there. I see you're going to be an asset to this class.' While the others wrote, she gave me a book with pictures. 'You'll come to my class as often as you like,' she said.

After geography I had to go back to Base, where I was told to sit beside a black-haired boy with deep-set eyes who stank of something unpleasant and threatened to kill me. Neither one of us could write and we were assigned to a special teacher, yet by the time I left that school, I still had not mastered the art.

My first few months at school were not happy. I believed that all the boys hated me except for a few, and that few included other ethnic minority kids. Two sons of Pakistani shopkeepers, a Chinese, a couple of black kids. Most of the girls, however, were friendly and hung around me. The teachers were great. But I was three times bullied; bullied because I was dark-skinned, bullied because I went to Base, bullied because I lived in the children's centre. I had stones thrown at me, I was spat at and called racist names; I was tripped up in the corridors; I was punched and kicked; I had pepper thrown in my face.

When I told a teacher, she took me to one side. 'We know what's going on, but we can't do anything about it. If we give them detention it'll make it worse. We're not allowed to punish them any other way. The best thing to do is just to smile, rise above it and ignore them. We'll try to be around as much as possible.'

They only knew some of it. One day it was so bad that I refused to go to school for three days.

Had this happened in Bangladesh these bullies would have felt the weight of the Imam's cane until they cringed and begged for mercy. Children of my own race treated newcomers with kindness and the teachers with respect. I could not understand the fact that those kids could not be punished.

I did not go to the tuck-shop at break time because of bullying outside the school gates and spent those minutes sitting against the school wall.

One day the janitor came up to me. 'I've been watching you. You're not having an easy time, are you, mate?'

I stared at the ground and shook my head.

'Look, come to my office, I've got enough food for two.'

I thanked him very much. He introduced himself as Duncan and gave me a cup of tea and a biscuit and asked me how I was getting on at school.

'I don't like it. I'm learning nothing and the other boys don't like me.'

'From now on, come to my office every break time.'

After that, I spent a lot of time with the janitor and he became a very good friend. But the bullying still continued both at school and at the centre.

'You'll be happier in Glasgow once we get it arranged,' said John. 'There are children of all races and religions there and the homes are better able to meet your needs. But we'll have to get a proper date of birth for you. Once we've got that we can move forward. You'll need another examination in the hospital.'

A couple of days later, John took me to the hospital where I had another long, embarrassing examination.

I couldn't understand what was so important about a date of birth.

Slowly I began to fit in at school. I loved sport and was now playing my beloved cricket regularly. Surprised by my skill in badminton, Ms Nichol asked me if I would coach the younger children. I was only too pleased to do that.

To my delight, Kirsty and her friends stayed close to me, but so too did Hamish and his, and whenever he had the chance, his persecution was relentless. I remembered my Abboo's words, 'Violence breeds violence,' so each time he hurt me I smiled at him and thanked him. He stared at me as if I was crazy, but it worked. Eventually, he lost interest.

Then one day John told me I didn't have to go back to school. He told me they had issued a new birth certificate for me and supplied a date of birth.

'You're going to Glasgow.' As he spoke he smiled, as if he expected me to be pleased. At that moment I realised that I didn't want to leave. I wanted to teach badminton to the younger kids, many of whom I'd already grown fond of and who accepted me as an equal, I wanted to spend time next summer with my janitor friend. Most of all, I didn't want to leave Kirsty and the other kids who were kind to me.

'Let me go back to school,' I said, desperate to see her before I left.

John looked surprised. 'I thought you hated that school.'

'Things are changing.' I stared at the window and the rain running down the pane. 'I don't want to leave.'

The next day Kirsty arrived at the school gates at the same time as I did. She ran up to me and grabbed my hand. 'I'm so happy to see you.'

'I'm happy to see you too,' I said.

She grinned showing her perfect teeth and kissed my cheek. Shocked, I stepped back and quickly turned from her. Girls in Bangladesh would never be so forward.

Her face crumpled and she stormed away, stamping her feet. Hurting her had been the last thing I wanted to do. I ran after her. 'Sorry,' I said, 'it's different where I come from. I like you, but I don't know what to do.' A few kids nearby heard me and laughed.

Kirsty studied me for a moment, then her face relaxed and her lips spread in a wide grin. She was such a pretty girl, my heart went soft.

'It's ok,' she said. 'Give me a hug.' She threw her arms around me and, thinking this was what I was meant to do, I hugged her back. It was as if a charge shot through me. I had never been hugged by a young girl who was not my sister and it raised a range of new feelings, both good and frightening.

The other kids cheered and laughed.

'Don't mind them.' She flicked her hair back, her eyes shining.

'I've... I've something to tell you.' I swallowed and my mouth was dry.

'Yes?' She gazed expectantly into my eyes.

'I'm going away.'

Her expression changed as if a thundercloud had covered the sun. 'Away...you can't...where?'

'Glasgow. This is my last day at school.'

The light vanished from her eyes, she spun from me and marched away, her shoulders back, her head high, gleaming hair feathering in the breeze behind her.

'I don't want to go,' I shouted after her.

She didn't speak to me again all day.

That night I packed my bag slowly. I was leaving for Glasgow next morning and the thought of going once more into the unknown scared me.

'Don't look so sad,' said John. 'You'll love it there.'

'I love it here. I've got friends now and I've got you and the rest of the staff. I don't want to go.'

'I thought you'd be glad. You'll be away from that lot out there.' He jerked his head towards the door.

'I suppose.' I stared at my hands twisting in my lap. I didn't care. I didn't want to leave.

Kathy shoved her head around the door. 'Abdul, there's a girl out there asking for you.' She raised her eyebrows.

My face grew hot. It had to be Kirsty.

Outside it was raining. Kirsty stood on the front step, hood up, hands in her pockets. She lifted her head, the raindrops ran down her cheeks and tendrils of her hair stuck to her forehead. 'I'll miss you,' she whispered.

'I'll miss you too,' I replied. And I knew I would. I wanted to tell her that it was her friendship that had made my life at school bearable and how much that had meant to me, but words failed me.

Drops of water gathered on her lips and she licked them away. 'Come out with me.'

'I wish ... I wish I could. I'm not allowed.'

'Just ask.'

'Ten minutes,' said Kathy. 'Remember, I'm trusting you.'

We walked to the nearest shop and bought sweets. The rain drummed against the hood of my jacket and soaked my jeans and shoes, yet being this close to Kirsty lifted my spirits. Ten minutes. Not long to say goodbye. We stood awkwardly on the step in front of the home.

'Cheerio,' she said and kissed my cheek again. Her lips were cold and wet. I hoped she would hug me, but she just stood there, damp and dejected looking.

I wondered if I should hug her, but decided against it.

'Abdul,' is that you?' Kathy, opened the door. 'Come away in before you catch your death.'

'Goodbye, Kirsty.' My heart had not felt this heavy

since I left Bangladesh. I could still see her shadow behind the glass of the door once it was shut.

'There'll be many more girls,' said Kathy softly.

The next morning, I sat on my bed with my bag on my lap, waiting for one of the staff to come and get me. Outside the wind had picked up and whistled around the building dragging raindrops sideways across the pane.

John came for me.

I stood up and slung the strap of my holdall over my shoulder.

Once more I was ready to walk into the unknown.

# Chapter 27

John slid his hand over his hair. 'Sit down, lad.' He shut the door behind him.

I lowered myself onto the bed.

He sat beside me and set his hands on his knees.

I clung to my holdall, my fists shut so tight that my knuckles shone white. Something was wrong. Several possibilities raced through my mind. I was going home to Bangladesh, or my worst nightmare, I was going to be sent back to Hoss.

The seconds stretched and fizzled between us. I could hear my heart beat all the way up to my neck.

John smiled. 'Don't look so anxious.'

I pulled air into my lungs.

'Do you really want to stay?'

'You know I do.'

'Well, I just got an email from the powers that be. If you really want to stay, you can.'

'Really?' I couldn't believe it. 'I can stay here?' I threw my holdall on the floor and sprung to my feet, an uncontrollable and genuine smile on my face. I wanted to hug John.

'I argued your case. I told them you'd made friends and didn't need to be unsettled again. It wasn't easy, but in the end they agreed.'

'Oh, thank you, thank you. I won't let you down – I'll go to school every day. I'll ....'

'Hold on,' said John with a laugh. 'It's not all for your sake, you know. You're like a ray of sunshine with that ready smile. We'd miss you too.'

I was so happy. I wanted to tell Kirsty but didn't know how to reach her at that moment. I made up my mind to go to school every day, to stand up to the bullies, rise above it, not let them get me down.

Later a young woman called Beth, came to see me. 'We need to keep you away from that lot as much as possible.' She indicated with her head at the door. 'My parents are good Christians and their church runs an activity club. We would like you to go there in the evenings.'

'A Christian church?' I asked, wondering if this was a ploy to convert me.

'I know you're Muslim, but you know what? I've converted to Islam too.'

'You have?' I looked up with interest.

She gave a little laugh. 'With all the unrest in the Middle East, I wanted to see what it was really about, so some of my classmates in the university and myself, we took to studying the Qur'an and we discovered that men have twisted its meaning to suit their own ends. It's a good religion. A lot of my friends felt the same way. But if Muslims want to convert the world, it will be with love and example, not force.'

I was surprised by her words. 'But your parents...'.

'My parents don't mind. They brought me up to be my own person. I pray in my own room. The rest of the staff don't know; they mightn't understand. So not a word, eh?'

'Yeah, sure.' I felt happiness swell in my chest. I was no longer isolated in my religion.

'There's bad people everywhere,' she said. 'But I believe there are more good people in the world than bad, and you, Abdul, are one of the good ones.' She touched my hand and her smile was so kind and genuine that I felt surrounded by a warmth similar to that which the dreams of the old man brought to me.

I thought of my own parents, and how my Abboo had brought me up to believe that we must love all nations and be tolerant of all religions. He would not mind me going to activities in a Christian church.

That night I was allowed to go out for a short walk alone. 'Just to the nearest shop and back,' said Kathy. 'Then maybe tomorrow you'll get out a bit longer.' For the second time I was trusted to go out without being supervised.

The first night Beth took me to the church youth club, it was very different from walking into the school. It was good there. I was made welcome. From the beginning I was surprised that our religions were so similar. Everyone in the hall was friendly and made me feel comfortable. The night started with a prayer where we bowed our heads and clasped our hands and gave thanks to God and asked for food and comfort for the poor and unhappy and for peace in the world. Then we had a short lesson about the love of Jesus Christ. After that we played a game of football and drank juice. There were other games, billiards and computer games. We finished the night with another prayer. My nights at the church activities taught me the similarity of our two religions. Both believed in the basics of decency, honesty and compassion, both taught a moral and clean lifestyle. I am glad I had the opportunity to learn these things. I have also since met many good people from many different beliefs, yet they, too, are good people.

After the first visit, I was allowed to go alone. One night, on my way back to the home, I came across a group of kids standing inside a shop doorway, laughing and joking. Unsure, and afraid of abuse, I tried to skirt around them.

One of them called to me. 'You're Abdul, aren't you?'
I nodded.
'I'm Calumn. This here's Kevin.' He pointed to the girls. 'Katie and Mia. What year are you in?'
'Second,' I said.
'We are in the fifth,' Kevin said.

Katie had dark hair and big brown eyes and she reminded me of A'isha, or how she would have looked with white skin. Katie reached out and touched my face. 'What a lovely colour you are. It would cost me a fortune on the sunbed to get that colour. I'm so jealous.'

'What?' I couldn't believe that someone would be jealous of my skin and thought she must be making fun of me.

'I use fake tan,' said Mia. 'You should see the colour of my sheets.'

'I would like to see your sheets,' said Calumn, and Mia punched his arm playfully.

Kevin laughed. 'That's the girls round here for you, Abdul, always wanting what they don't have.'

I realised then that the kids were not making fun of me. 'Come on,' said Calumn. 'Come down town with us.'

'Please,' said Mia, smiling sweetly.

But I had been trusted to come straight back to the centre and had to leave them there.

The next day was Saturday. Kevin and Calumn called at the centre and asked me out with them, but it was Kathy's day off and her stand-in would not allow me to leave.

'I'm sorry,' I said to my new friends, 'This place is like a prison.'

At school on Monday, at break time, Calumn and Kevin came looking for me, and invited me to join them in a game of football. From then on, they became my protectors from the bullies and my very good friends.

Then, one night, John called me into the office. 'We're taking you to Glasgow again to see your solicitor. They need a signature for the immigration people. If all goes well, you should be free to stay in this country.'

'I don't want an interpreter. My English is good enough.' I couldn't risk meeting another of Hoss's friends.

'I hoped you say that.' John steepled his fingers. 'There's not many interpreters from Syhlet in Scotland and I guess, Hoss can get to any of them.'

It was a long drive to Glasgow and we booked into a hotel for the night. I shared a room with Bill. Again the night terrors overtook me and I woke sweating and fighting with the duvet. The black shadows still reached out to me in my mind, the sharp cutters closed round my finger and I saw the blood everywhere, dripping from the ceiling, splattered on the walls of the dark, dirty room of the Hell-House. I heard children cry and footsteps heavy in the corridor and knew they were coming to get me next. I buried my face in the pillow so as not to wake Bill.

Suddenly the room flooded with light. I opened my eyes and Bill was propped up on one elbow staring at me. 'What's wrong?' he asked.

'I'm sorry, I'm sorry,' I cried, holding myself against the fear that always stayed with me on waking. 'I didn't mean to disturb you.' Uncontrollable tears rolled down my cheeks, making me ashamed. I hid my face in my hands and stifled the sobs.

'Don't be sorry. What was it?'

'Nothing. Sorry. Bad dream.'

'That was more than a bad dream. You sounded as if someone was killing you.'

Shaking, I blinked myself fully awake. Glad of the light, glad of Bill's presence.

'I'm sorry,' I croaked.

'How long have you been having nightmares?'

'Always. Most nights.'

'Why on earth didn't you tell someone?'

'What can you do? No one can mend my mind.'

'They can, Abdul. You can be helped.'

'You can help me?' Was it really possible that I could finally sleep in peace? This sounded like magic.

'Of course,' said Bill. 'We'll sort it when we go home. You can talk to someone, but you'll have to tell them everything.'

Everything? No, I could never tell everything as long as Hoss was free.

# Chapter 28

The meeting with my solicitor went well. She explained the immigration process and all that had to be considered. 'Read your statement over and sign it.' She pushed the document towards me. This time I asked, 'When can I go back to Bangladesh?' She explained that I could do nothing until I was eighteen.

I looked at the document before me and shook my head. 'I can't read.'

She pulled it back. 'I'll read it to you.'

When she had finished, I took the pen and, with a shaking hand, I signed my name. 'Does this mean I must stay in Scotland?'

'It's not up to me. But we're almost there.'

Once we returned to the centre, I was introduced to a counsellor who asked me questions about my dreams. I wanted help to stop the dreams and answered her questions as fully as I could.

'Your problems are too complex for me,' she said, standing up. 'You will need to be referred further.'

It took a week to set me up with a psychiatrist in Inverness. I could never totally unburden myself. Hoss had the power to have my parents killed if he found out that I had betrayed him in any way.

However, talking about my nightmares, bringing them out into the open and exposing them to the light of day eventually diminished them, made them seem less real.

For two and a half years I spent weekly sessions with either a psychologist or a psychiatrist, but while my brain healed and my waking hours became less troubled, the night terrors did not disappear altogether. Now the old man appeared more often and each time he stayed a little longer. And I spoke to him, asked him questions which he only answered in riddles. Yet the peace he radiated enveloped me more and more. I prayed daily and, each night, I held the locket, comforted in the knowledge that my ammo's hands had once held it too.

I spoke about the old man to my psychiatrist.

Not long after, I was told that I may be suffering from *schizophrenia*. My psychiatrist explained what that meant, and said medication would help. Surely that was too good to be true? A tablet would take away my terrors, allow me a night's sleep? My hopes were short lived. I was on medication for four years and it did nothing for me at all. We continued with the therapy, which helped only a little.

The children's centre was my home for two years. I got on well with the staff and some of the kids, but others continued to make my life hell. Eventually I was not only accepted at school, but became popular and made many good friends. Apart from badminton, I joined other clubs, karate, football, cricket, squash and basketball. I went skiing and took music lessons. I managed to get a part time job in a local fish and chip shop. Kirsty and I remained good friends. I went to the school discos with her and discovered that I loved to dance.

Bill did take me to meet his son, Finley, who went to a different school, and we became close. Finley played in a band and most Fridays I went along with him, returning late. On these nights, I was allowed to stay over at his house.

By now I was trusted to go and come as I pleased and I felt more settled, but I missed my family desperately. In spite of having many good friends who might have helped me, I was still afraid to tell anyone the truth. I saved up my money to buy myself a phone. This was something to look forward to, to dream about, being able to speak to them again. I had so much to tell them.

I was building a life.

Then, one night, that life came crashing round my ears.

Sometimes when I was out in town with my friends, I stopped to chat to some other guys from Bangladesh who worked in a restaurant in the High Street. One night as we passed the restaurant, one of the waiters came out and invited me inside. 'Someone wants to speak to you.'

A cold, prickly sensation began at the base of my neck. 'Who?' Visions from the past flashed before my eyes.

'On the telephone,' the guy said.

I stepped inside the foyer, suspecting who it would be even before I heard the voice, and yet I went, still a mindless puppet.

'So you are no longer guarded,' said Hoss.

I went numb.

The cold, hard voice continued. 'Did they tell you I phoned the children's home? They wouldn't let me talk to you.'

'No one told me,' I lied. 'How did you find me?'

He laughed. 'You think it's difficult? You can't run from me. I phoned every Indian restaurant in the Highlands and asked for a list of children's homes in the area. All I had to do was phone each home in turn and ask for you. Most had never heard of you. The minute someone asked who I was and said you weren't allowed phone calls, I knew where you were.'

'I can't run away, they'll find me.' I spoke through dry lips.

You could if you wanted. I've had you watched, you little shit. I thought I'd tell you that, because of you, your parents are dead. I had them killed. Slit their throats – cut their heads right off.' He laughed. 'They bled like pigs. I hope you're satisfied. I'm coming for you next.'

216

I flung the phone from me and turned to run out, my heart exploding, but the waiter was barring the way. Another grabbed my arms. 'Hoss wants you back,' he said. 'You owe him money.'

My friends heard my shouts as I fought against my captors. Kevin hurled a stone through the window. With a roar, the waiter flung the door open and ran outside after him. In the commotion, I broke free, pushed past him and ran with my friends along the street, down the lane and into the darkness of the riverside. The street was quiet that night, there were no witnesses and the incident was never reported to the police. I was so upset, shaking like a leaf in the wind, I imagined that my legs had turned to jelly.

'They've killed my parents,' I repeated over and over again. Even the tears would not come. My heart was like to burst.

One of my friends went away and returned with a bottle of vodka. 'Drink this. Honestly, it'll calm you.'

By then I couldn't speak, but still shook my head. Alcohol is forbidden for Muslims.

Kevin spoke. 'You'll feel better.' He opened the bottle and handed it to me.

I knew he was a kind and caring person, a good person, and he only had my interest at heart.

Looking at my friend's concerned face, I took the bottle. I drank. I coughed against the burn, but I didn't care anymore and continued to drink until the burn faded and I began to feel different, strange. That night, for the first time in my life, I got drunk. And for the first time, I was punished when I returned to the centre. I staggered into the home, falling against the wall. The alcohol had loosened my emotions and all I could do was cry.

The form of punishment favoured in this country is 'grounding,' which meant I was imprisoned in the centre for a week and lost all my privileges.

I did not tell anyone in the centre about what had happened, what had made me take the vodka, as they would have locked me up again for my own safety and I didn't want to lose my freedom for longer than the duration of my 'grounding.'

That restaurant was closed shortly after when the owner was arrested for a different incident. It never opened again and is now a completely different business.

After that I lost myself. Believing my parents were dead, I was devastated. It was impossible to find a place where I belonged. I had been removed from my own culture when I was ten and had forgotten so much. I had now lived in Britain for almost as many years as I had lived in Bangladesh and my Britishness would make it difficult to fit in my own country, yet, because of my Bangladeshi roots, I did not belong in the British culture either. I no longer associated with the local Muslim community as I believed Hoss could get to any of them. I had no family. No one to call my own.

In spite of all I had been through, I had always clung to my faith and the belief that one day I would return and be reunited with Ammo and Abboo and my siblings. Never before had I felt so isolated and alone. My life took a downward spiral. My good friends became my lifeline.

Life in the centre continued to be hard. The staff were kind, but the number of kids coming and going made it impossible to form lasting relationships. But the bullies did not move on and all the hatred trapped inside them was directed towards me. I now had my mobile phone and Kathy told me to call her if anyone tried to break into my room. Outsiders judged me as being bad as the centre was a place for disruptive teens. Decent kids, sent there through no fault of their own, were soon placed with foster families. My friends on the outside all had homes and parents and, seeing them within their family life, I remembered my own and longed to be part of something again. Finally I asked if I could be fostered as well.

The staff at the home agreed that would be for the best and put the wheels in motion. My social workers also were supportive of my request and John asked me to dictate and sign a letter to the head of Social Work department to strengthen the request.

*26th March 2004*
*Dear Miss \*\*\*\*\*\*\**
*I am writing to tell you that I am not happy living at the children's centre. There are lots of problems for me there.*

*1. Another boy who lives at the centre calls me names, swears at me and my friends.*

*2. The other ones in the centre kick my door (sometimes in the night) and play loud music at night when I am trying to sleep.*

*3. The other boy last week grabbed my clothes and neck and told me 'You will soon be dead'. He has done this before. He has tried to steal some of my things from me like my mobile phone.*

*4. One day the lock was broken on my room door. People have been in my room.*

*5. I lie in bed at night worrying about these other people. I don't feel safe.*

*6. People think that because I am living at the centre I must be a bad boy. Last week my friend's mum asked me why I lived at the centre. I tried to explain to her but she said, 'You are a drug dealer. Don't speak to my daughter again.' This hurt me.*

*7. Although I am allowed to have school friends visit me at the centre they do not want to come because of the bad reputation of some of the boys there.*

*8. I am not allowed to stay at other people's houses overnight. My friends' families wonder why I'm not allowed to do this and some think it is because I am a bad boy.*

*I like all the staff at the centre, but please help me find a foster family.*

*I don't want to live in another centre because I love this town. I have friends at school and the staff are like a family to me. I would hate to be sent anywhere else.*

*Yours Sincerely*
*Abdul Mkith (sic)*

The letter must have done the trick as not long after that I got my wish.

Kathy came to find me. 'I have a surprise for you, Abdul. I want you to come and meet your new foster family. They are in the office.'

At that moment I was filled with such hope. I was going to get a family of my own. I walked into the office and I was introduced to an older couple. The man clasped my hand in a firm handshake that filled me with confidence. He said, 'How're you doing, son?'

I answered politely. But it was the woman who really drew my attention. She was small and smiling and appeared to radiate a warm glow. When she clasped my hand that glow filled me up. I would have gladly gone home with them then and there, but she explained that she had no room for me at present. 'You can come and stay with us at the weekends, when the others go home to their parents,' she said.

I was so disappointed. Four weekends later, one of their other foster kids moved on, and they had a room for me. I was free again, leaving dread in my wake, flying towards another chapter of my life.

The only blot on my horizon was, now that I was out of the centre, it might be easier for Hoss to get to me. I constantly looked over my shoulder. As time passed I waited for Hoss to try something else, and when it didn't happen, I began to wonder whether he had as much power as he would have me believe.

On my first night in my new home, I had another nightmare. I woke up screaming and the old man was sitting in a chair grinning at me. 'Are you comfortable now?' he said. When Granny came through to see what was wrong, I told her there was someone in my room.

'Ah,' she said, 'we know of him. It's our resident ghost. We call him Angus, but don't worry, he won't hurt you.'

Ghost? No this was not Angus, this was my old man, but I couldn't explain why this time he frightened me. Maybe because I had not seen him for so long, I thought I no longer needed him. The episode made me realise he would always be with me. However, the very fact that I was believed made me feel comforted.

Finally I was part of a family again. My foster parents accepted me with their whole hearts and, with their help and support, my life completely changed around. Now I was no longer a 'Centre Kid', I had a family of my own who lived in a big house, I had my own spacious room and my new family involved me in any choice of decor. I was allowed to have friends over, and subsequently became more accepted by their families. Granny and Grandad are still my Scottish family till this day. What I am now has been all down to their love and care.

I was treated like their own son, and given every benefit, but I still wasn't sleeping well at night. In the morning I could hardly drag myself out of bed.

Granny grew fed up with trying to pull me awake every morning and one day she lost her temper. 'What is the matter with you?' she shouted. 'Why can't you ever get up in the morning?' It was the first time she'd raised her voice to me. I lost control and burst into tears. When I finally caught myself, I opened up and, between sobs, I told her all about my nightmares.

Oh, Abdul.' She cried with me and put her arms around me and I felt secure, as if for the first time in my life, I was going to be safe.

Most nights, when the others had gone to bed, I lay on the couch while she sat across from me, and we talked long into the night about everything and anything. These talks still mean so much to me. She is my second mother and my best friend.

On my sixteenth birthday, Granny asked me if I'd ever had a cake.

'Cake, no, why should I have a cake?' I asked.

'Well this year, you'll have a cake,' she said. She baked me a huge cake, and invited all of her family over. They were all so kind to me. I was so happy that day.

With my part-time job, I was making some money of my own and I saved as much as I could. The desire to speak to someone from home grew until it consumed me – I needed to know what had happened to my parents – how they died, where my siblings were.

All I could remember of my early calls to Bangladesh was the number of digits. Although I still struggled with reading and writing, I had always been good with numbers and found it easy to carry them in my head. However, since I had not telephoned home in so long, most of those numbers had either slipped away or become jumbled in my mind. Being unable to read or write, I could not use a computer or telephone directory. I knew nothing of directory enquiries at that time. Why didn't I ask one of my good friends or my new family for help in locating the numbers? Truth was I still could not fully trust anyone with my secret. Secrets and lies had been branded into my brain so that phoning home, too, had to be kept hidden. I didn't know what else to do. Yet now my parents really were dead, and all because of me.

I began to phone random numbers. I spent all my wages and pocket money on credit.

Each time someone answered I asked them where they lived and what country they were in. I must have phoned millions of numbers before I got someone in Bangladesh. Finally, I had a country code. Now I had to get an area code. Again I tried hundreds of numbers. By this method I finally reached my home district of Syhlet. It was so frustrating as I kept running out of credit and had to wait until I had more money. In total, my quest took me four years. Eventually, I was so near I could taste success. I had both the country code and the area code. Then, when I had almost used up all my credit and barely had enough for one more call before I had to save up again, a miracle happened.

'Sharma's law practice,' said the soft female voice that answered in my home dialect. My heart raced. A Mr Sharma had a law practice in my village, close to my father's shop.

'My name is Abdul Mkith,' I began. Before I could say more, the lady on the other end of the line shrieked. 'Abdul Mkith? Chanu's son?'

'Yes,'

'We thought you were dead. Wait there until I get your father.'

'You mean he's still alive?' At that second my credit ran out and my phone died.

My hands shook. My heart was like to burst from my chest. My father was not dead. Surely, somehow, a lawyer would be able to trace the number from which the call was made. Surely, somehow, they would find the means to call me back. I sat where I was, on a bench by the river. People passed, walking dogs, or taking a stroll. Traffic sounded in the distance. There was a faraway rumble of thunder. A train chuffed into the station at the other side of the river. Some time later, it chuffed out again. The phone did not ring.

To wait a week until I got my next wage was so hard. I begged fifty pounds from my foster mother. She didn't ask me why I needed it, but handed me the money anyway. I put every penny into credit.

When Mrs Sharma answered, I dropped the receiver in my excitement. My trembling hand grabbed at it and pressed it to my ear. 'Hello,' I answered. 'This is Abdul Mkith.'

The sun sank and the midges, Scotland's own brand of mosquitos, feasted on my skin, but I barely noticed. Time slowed down although my heart raced. At last my ammo's voice shook down the miles. 'Abdul, Abdul,' she said, then she couldn't speak for crying. Abboo came on the phone. 'My son,' he said and he too cried. My voice dried. I was so glad of the seat beneath me for my legs would not have had the strength to hold me up.

'Where are you?' Abboo asked.

'Scotland.'

'Where is that? Why did you leave England?'

'Scotland is part of Britain, same as England.'

'You've been there all this time?'

'Of course. How are my brothers and sisters?'

'They have all gone. When we could no longer reach you, Mr Hossain told us you had run away and gone to another country. They have all gone to other countries looking for you among Bangladeshi communities. We've been so worried.'

Tears ran unheeded down my cheeks, tickling like ants. Afraid of my credit running out again, I gave him my number.

After that we spoke almost daily. I told them about the kind family with whom I lived, of how I had learned that the power of good and evil struggles within every race and in every religion and even in those who had no religion at all. How I believed that was my purpose, to know about those matters. But I told them nothing of the bad things that had happened to me, I could never put them through the pain of knowing what they had sent me to. Not then. Not ever.

It was after that I decided to write this book. It was only when I made a Data Subject Access via Disclosure Scotland request and received all the files held on me, that I found out the extent to which Hoss had gone to get me back in his clutches.

When his own efforts failed, someone with an Asian accent had phoned the authorities saying that they were updating files on all the children's homes in the Area. It was considered too much of a coincidence, and no information was given.

Hoss then hired a lawyer, demanding my return.

When I heard the reports in the file held on me by the authorities. I discovered that the interpreter, undoubtedly schooled by Hoss and too afraid not to obey, lied and told them Hoss's version.

The story he had reported as having been told to him by me, was a total fabrication.

He had told them that I had only arrived in January 2003 (I was rescued in June that year.)

He also said that I had lost my finger in Bangladesh during an attack by the Mafia, and in that same attack, my father was killed. He then gave a made-up version of how I arrived in the UK.

He had carried on to give a glowing account of my opinion of Hoss

*Quote; Abdul describes Mr Hossain as a good man, giving him lots of money and clothes. Abdul refers to Mr*

*Hossain as uncle, although he is no blood relative.*

*The term 'uncle' is believed to be a mark of respect rather than a reference to an actual relative.*

*Signed and dated (sic)*

This story was not believed by the authorities however, There were too many inconsistencies.

*Quote; Mr Hossain is not a relative of Abdul's but has taken a lot of interest in his welfare. Despite the current location of Abdul being kept confidential, Mr Hossain has managed to locate him and has been warned by the police not to make any contact with Abdul. He seems to be especially concerned with what Abdul has told the authorities.*

*The interest shown by Mr Hossain is of serious concern. Immigration has warned the unit to be cautious of him as they have prior knowledge of his activities. (sic)*

The final update was a lot more positive, however.

*Abdul is a very active and popular member of the local community in which he lives. He has an excellent school record and is currently undertaking 5th year studies. As a looked-after child he has a Personal Education Plan which is reviewed six monthly to address his individual and educational needs.*

*He has a part time job where he is viewed as a valuable member of staff who is hard working, polite and respectable. He is a very sociable person who has many friends in the area. (sic)*

# Chapter 29

There are balloons and streamers hanging from the ceiling. A banner is stretched across the front of the stage and big red letters proclaim the words ' Happy Birthday Abdul'

The huge ball in the middle of the dancehall rotates and reflects the flashing lights as the disc jockey prepares his equipment. The room is filled with all my friends, and many of my teachers, who clap their hands and sing *"Happy birthday to you"* as I walk through the doorway.

The strains of the song fill the air and when it finished, everyone cheers. The girls are dressed in pretty dresses and all look so beautiful. They come up and hug me and kiss me on the cheek. The boys slap me on the shoulder or give me high fives. Our hands whack together

At the end of the hall is a long table laden with food. There is even a cake with eighteen candles which I am told I must blow out. If I can do this with one blow, I can make a wish.

I cannot wish that my parents and siblings could see me now. They would not approve of the alcohol so freely consumed. Instead I close my eyes and blow, wishing with all my heart that I could watch Hoss bleed, that I could see his face when he meets the full force of the law. Then I am struck with a pang of guilt. It is written that Muslims must not seek revenge. I run out of breath, open my eyes and two candles still remain lit. There is a communal sigh. Someone presses a drink into my hand, the music starts and Kirsty is pulling me up onto the floor. The music flows through me and I feel the beat in my pulse and the party continues.

At the end of the night several boys hoist me onto their shoulders and everyone sings *"For he's a jolly good fellow"* as they carry me around the room.

Then they cheer. I am popular. I am accepted. For that moment in time I am so happy.

But my story isn't over. Not by a long way.

I must go home to Bangladesh. To see my family and friends again, to walk along the path through the paddy fields beneath the mango trees and everyone will know that Chanu's youngest son has returned. I must learn again of my own culture. But I will return to Britain and I will, one day, come face to face with Hoss again – this time on my terms.

With all the evil I have encountered, I still marvel that I was never raped. That final degradation might have irretrievably broken my spirit. I can only believe that my prayers and my continuing faith protected me.

Scotland is my home now; I have work here. And although they are not of my blood, I have a much loved family here.

# Update

I had been so happy on my eighteenth birthday, but my happiness was short lived. With the help of a scribe, I was doing well at school. I gave up my part time job in order to concentrate on my studies. My teachers were happy with me and were confident I could do well. That was before the bombshell.

My foster family received a letter telling them that since I was eighteen they would no longer get an allowance for me. I was also told I was no longer allowed to go to school.

My teachers tried to argue my case, but at eighteen I was too old for high school. However, I could go to college. Because of my problems with reading and writing the college put me in a class for young people with learning difficulties, where I learned nothing, so I opted to leave.

The authorities now needed my foster placement for other children.

'You are an adult now,' I was told. 'You have to make your own way in life. We can't support you any longer.'

I moved into a flat with one of my friends until I got a place of my own. At this time I was receiving benefit of £50 a week and paying £35 for rent. My foster family were still buying me food, but even paying for electricity was beyond me. Apart from lack of money, I had never had to budget and cope on my own before. Those were skills that we were never taught. Finding employment was almost impossible.

Eventually Granny found me cold and hungry and at a very low point, my depression having returned.

'Come on, Abdul, get your things. I'm taking you home,' she said.

The social workers were not pleased. This couple was one of their best foster families. No child was too much of a challenge and they did not want to lose a room to someone who was no longer supported by the system, but Granny and Grandad were adamant.

'Abdul is coming home with us,' Granny said, and she would have no argument.

I was so grateful at that point and once again felt the love from this unique family surround me, and make me whole.

Eventually, I was lucky enough to get a job with the oil industry. I returned to Bangladesh in October 15$^{th}$ 2012. After an emotional reunion with my parents, I removed the locket from my neck and handed it to my mother. 'Here, Ammo,' I said. 'This is the locket you gave me, the locket that brought me safely back to you.'

She held it in her hand, kissed it and started to cry.

The whole village turned up to meet me, Hindu, Muslim, Christian, they came in droves until three o'clock in the morning. I found out later that Hoss had gone to my parents in Bangladesh and threatened to kill me unless they paid him a large amount of money. My parents had to sell everything they owned to be able pay him off. After that, he did not get in touch with them again, and they believed that I was dead anyway.

My brothers were already settled in America and eventually managed to get my family over to join them. There they are safe from the gangs and Hoss's threats and I am free to tell my story to the world.

I now have two families now, both of whom I love equally, but Scotland is my home.

Although being separated from my culture for many years

and being part of a non-religious family, I am a practising Muslim. I still suffer from occasional nightmares, and I still see the old man in my dreams. I suffer ongoing health problems caused by my treatment in the Hell-House. Although I lost the five taka note, I still have the locket which I will always treasure.

I now feel as if I have come full circle. I began my life in a loving, supportive family, who installed many values within me, and after all my suffering, my journey has brought me back to yet another loving family and a deeper understanding of mankind.

If you have enjoyed this book, please leave a review, and tell your friends.

## Other books by Catherine M Byrne

**Fiction**
**Historical**
Follow the Dove
The Broken horizon
The Road to Nowhere
Isa's Daughter

**Contemporary**
Song for an Eagle.

**Anthology**
Gone with the tide